LUCRETIA MOTT

LUCRETIA MOTT

A Guiding Light

Jennifer Fisher Bryant

William B. Eerdmans Publishing Company
Grand Rapids, Michigan / Cambridge, U.K.

© 1996 Wm. B. Eerdmans Publishing Co.
255 Jefferson Ave. S.E., Grand Rapids, Michigan 49503 /
P. O. Box 163, Cambridge CB3 9PU U.K.

Printed in the United States of America

02 01 00 99 98 97 96   7 6 5 4 3 2 1

Library of Congress Cataloging-in-Publication Data

Bryant, Jennifer.
Lucretia Mott: a guiding light / Jennifer Fisher Bryant.
p.   cm.
Includes bibliographical references.
Summary: Traces the life of Lucretia Mott, an active leader of the
abolitionist and feminist movements, from her humble roots in New
England to her days at a New York Quaker boarding school, and through
her decades of social service in Philadelphia.
ISBN 0-8028-5115-0 (alk. paper).
ISBN 0-8028-5098-7 (pbk.: alk. paper)
1. Mott, Lucretia, 1793-1880 — Juvenile literature. 2. Feminists — United
States — Biography — Juvenile literature. 3. Abolitionists — United
States — Biography — Juvenile literature. 4. Quakers — United
States — Biography — Juvenile literature. [1. Mott, Lucretia, 1793-1880.
2. Feminists. 3. Abolitionists. 4. Women — Biography.]
I. Title.
HQ1413.M68B79   1995
305.42′092 — dc20
[B]   95-39373
CIP
AC

A number of quotations in this volume are from *Valiant Friend: The Life of
Lucretia Mott,* copyright © 1980 by Margaret Hope Bacon and reprinted with
permission from Walker and Company, 435 Hudson Street, New York, NY
10014 (1-800-289-2553). All rights reserved.

This book is dedicated to my parents,
Charles and Elizabeth,
who encouraged my love of books
and my interest in history.

Contents

CHAPTER 1

What about the Women?

May 7, 1840, was a day that Lucretia Mott would remember forever. At forty-seven years of age, she had already accomplished more than most nineteenth-century women could hope to accomplish in a lifetime. She had been married for almost thirty years, had raised five children, had been a teacher, and was one of the most respected ministers of her time. She was recognized as a leader in the Philadelphia Branch of the Society of Friends (also known as Quakers) and played an increasingly dominant role in the American anti-slavery movement. It seemed that she had already lived a full life, one which had required her to carefully balance her spiritual, intellectual, and nurturing capacities.

Yet, as she boarded the sailing vessel *Roscoe,* which was bound for Liverpool, England, she felt as if she were on the threshold of something new. "Everything novel and of deep interest," she wrote in her diary.

1

"Captain very kind. . . . 32 cabin passengers . . . and all most companionable. . . . Much time spent on the sides of the ship . . . looking afar. . . . Good humor abounds."

Lucretia and her husband James had been chosen to represent the Philadelphia branch of the American Anti-Slavery Society at the first World's Anti-Slavery Convention in London. This was in response to an invitation from the British Anti-Slavery Society which read,

> Will you send your full proportion of delegates from the United States? They will receive a hearty and kind welcome. . . . It will be a meeting of extraordinary interest. Not of politicians nor statesmen, . . . but of philanthropists, of Christians, irrespective of names, sects, rank or colour, the genuine, unassuming but tried friends of freedom.

At first the invitation had seemed an open one, with no restrictions based on race, gender, or creed. Philadelphia and New England branches had promptly elected their delegates, including a number of women, one of whom was Lucretia Mott, and a black man, Charles Lennox Remond. In a subsequent invitation, however, U.S. delegates were referred to as "gentlemen," implying that only males were to have a voice (and a vote) at the convention.

Despite this subtle discouragement from the British,

Lucretia Mott was determined to attend. Since childhood, she had been known for her tenacity, her unwillingness to compromise on issues close to her heart. As a young girl, she had been hardworking and dutiful, but her frequent defiance of established Quaker customs had earned her the nickname "Long Tongue." She had asked her mother numerous questions: Why must we sit so still in silent meeting? Why can't I put bows on my shoes? Must we visit *all* of the relatives on First Days (Sundays)? "She's a spirited one!" her Grandmother Folger had observed. Lucretia's mother had agreed: "Yes, [and] she likes to give as good as she gets!"

Yet, as an adult, Lucretia remained true to her Quaker heritage and faith. Like all members of the Society of Friends (the formal name for the Quaker denomination), she believed that men and women were equal in the sight of God. "In Christ there is neither male nor female," she reminded congregations wherever she preached. "In the beginning [we] were created equal . . . [and] the laws given . . . by Jesus make no distinction."

Lucretia's husband, James, was an intelligent, freethinking man who shared her views on gender equality. Through the years, he lent his full support to her traveling ministry, riding with her over hundreds of miles to reach Friends in distant corners of the still-young United States. At each gathering, James would find a seat near the back of the meetinghouse and listen attentively to Lucretia's sermons, nodding his approval as she spoke.

3

In addition to interpreting the Gospel and extolling the virtues of Christian living, Lucretia frequently spoke in favor of abolition (passing laws to make slavery illegal). She believed that freedom was the right of all those living in America, and that slavery was a despicable evil: "Every man ha[s] a right to his own body," she told a New York congregation. "No man ha[s] a right to enslave or imbrute his brother, or to hold him for a moment as his property — to put a fellow-being on the auction-block, and sell him to the highest bidder." James supported her in this argument as well. When Lucretia encountered resistance because of such "radical" views, he quickly rose to her defense: "I am as opposed to slavery as anyone else and [I believe that] . . . gospel love . . . will bring acknowledgement [by the slaveowners] of this truth."

When the British learned that the Americans intended to include women in their delegation, they called upon Joseph Sturge, a prominent London abolitionist, to handle the matter. In a letter to the Philadelphia branch of the Anti-Slavery Society, he wrote, "The best for our cause, would be for you to do all you can to discourage it."

Lucretia ignored the warning, remaining firm in her conviction that women were equally suited to public life, equally capable of contributing to the progress in social reform. "I long for the time when my sisters will rise, and occupy the sphere to which they are called by their high nature and destiny," she later proclaimed.

Lucretia's decision incurred the disapproval of several American delegates, including a few from Philadelphia. There were others, however, who supported her wholeheartedly. William Lloyd Garrison, a newspaper editor who was one of the most widely respected abolitionists of the time, wrote, "I [cannot] . . . tell you how delighted I am to learn that you and James are soon to embark for England. . . . My heart leaped at the intelligence; for I could not be reconciled to the thought that you were to remain behind."

As the controversy surrounding Lucretia's attendance grew, so did her anticipation of the adventure. During the first days of the voyage, she was "humiliated" when seasickness forced her to remain below deck in her tiny cabin. (Because her father had been a sea captain, Lucretia had assumed that she would be immune to the physical effects of ocean voyages.) Though petite and delicately built, she weathered the discomfort with fortitude and cheerfulness.

When the illness had passed, she wandered about on deck, chatting amiably with the other passengers and crew members. John Greenleaf Whittier, a New England Quaker and the poet laureate of the abolitionist movement, had once described her as "singularly beautiful in appearance, dressed in the plain but not inelegant garb of a Friend." When she spoke, her words were always "well-chosen," and she took great interest in everything being discussed.

At night, Lucretia would record the day's events in

her diary: "[May 13], 1840: . . . Tremendous sea, sublime view — Much interesting conversation on slavery . . . on Theology . . . on Politics . . . [but] no conversions — 'bread cast upon the waters'. . . . Hymns sung frequently."

The *Roscoe* docked in Liverpool on May 27, the crossing having taken nearly three weeks. The Motts, along with the rest of the American delegation, "took a leisurely ten days to reach London, stopping . . . on the way [to see] the sights." Freed temporarily from the constant demands made by family, church, and social-welfare organizations back in Philadelphia, Lucretia was relaxed and in good humor. She joked frequently with her traveling companions and relished simple pleasures like good food and stimulating conversation. In a diary entry made during this unhurried trip, she reveals her sense of humor, her intellectual curiosity, and her childlike delight in new experiences: "May 28th: . . . Visit[ed] [an] English cottage, handsome grounds — fine garden — much conversation on . . . factory system — women's duties and responsibilities. . . . Man inquired if that OLD lady crossed the Atlantic! . . . Everything in first rate style and order. . . . [They] enclose bread in napkins at dinner. . . . Soup & fish removed before meats brought on; one kind of vegetable offered at a time. . . . Tea always made at table. . . . Nice!"

Once settled in a rooming house on Queen Street Place in London, the Motts were visited by Joseph Sturge. He pleaded with Lucretia on behalf of the British abolitionists who were opposed to admitting women delegates to the convention. Lucretia stood her ground and had the full support of her husband and several other New England abolitionists. Nevertheless, in the week preceding the convention, she received many letters of protest and was the subject of a few angry speeches by the British on "the proper sphere of women."

The situation was further complicated by certain members of the British Society of Friends. Upon learning that Lucretia and James belonged to the liberal branch of the Friends known as the "Hicksites," conservative English Quakers did their best to discredit them. According to biographer Margaret Hope Bacon, "They had heard that [Lucretia] was a radical even among the Hicksites, mingling freely with Unitarian ministers [Quakers do not hire ministers, as Unitarians do] and preaching more and more forcefully a simple gospel of love and good works that to many ears was nothing less than a denial of the divinity of Christ."

Despite such criticism, at the end of the week Lucretia announced her intention to attend the convention. On June 12, she was among the first to arrive at Freemason's Hall. True to their word, however, the British recognized only male delegates, forcing all females present, including duly elected Lucretia Mott, to sit behind a railing that separated them from the rest of the convention participants.

Veteran English abolitionist Thomas Clarkson gave

a moving opening speech, calling for an immediate end to "the horrors" of slavery. This was followed by a motion from one of the American delegates that women be admitted to the proceedings. A heated debate over "the woman question" ensued. Several American delegates, including James Mott and young Henry Stanton (a delegate from Boston), spoke in favor of the proposal. They were joined by a British lawyer who declared that it was "ridiculous to call it a World Convention and then exclude half the world."

Despite this and other forceful arguments in favor of women's participation in the convention, the opposition remained unmoved. When a final vote was taken, ninety percent of the delegates voted against the proposal. Lucretia's heart sank. She "wondered if she ought to continue at all under the circumstances." But others in attendance, both male and female, encouraged her to remain visible throughout the week's proceedings. In a letter to her daughters, Lucretia wrote, "Seeing . . . how altogether unprecedented it is for women to be admitted . . . in business meetings, [I am] disposed to regard it as one great step in the history of world reform."

At the time, Lucretia could not know the extent to which her presence at the convention would motivate other women to stand up for themselves and claim a voice in the public arena. Likewise, she could not know how deeply the rejection of women from the London meeting would later affect her own views on women's rights in America. At the close of the convention, Lucretia wrote that she and several other women "resolved to hold a convention . . . [when] we return home, and form a society to advocate the rights of women."

It was a promise she would not forget.

CHAPTER 2

An Island Childhood

The island lay silent in the pale gray dawn of the New England winter. A pair of seagulls circled lazily over the shoreline where the icy January wind whipped the Atlantic into a foamy froth. Drifting inward, the gulls came to rest on the roof of an oak-framed house, nestled among a dozen similar dwellings lining Fair Street. A soft, glowing light from the interior shone through the clear glass windowpanes, its shadows dancing across the boxwood bushes in the front yard.

Inside, Thomas Coffin Jr. bent his tall, lean figure over the hearth, carefully stoking the fire with long pieces of driftwood that his wife had gathered on the Nantucket beaches. Two-year-old Sarah remained close to his side, handing him smaller branches from the woodpile. When the job was finished, Thomas sat down on a hard wooden chair. Lifting Sarah gently onto his lap, he settled down once again to wait.

Upstairs, Thomas's wife Anna lay in bed, anticipating

the birth of their second child. She was tired, but she sensed that the time for delivery was near. Pushing aside a strand of her dark-brown hair, she smiled at the midwife, Rachael Bunker, whose job it was to was keep Anna comfortable through the labor and to bring both mother and child safely through the birth.

As the morning light filtered in through the lace curtains, Anna's contractions came more rapidly. Within the hour, she was cradling her second daughter, Lucretia, in her arms.

"Mighty skinny!" Rachael commented. "I hope thou'll be able to raise her." After summoning Thomas and Sarah, she left the three of them alone to spend a few moments with the newest member of their family.

Nantucket, the community into which Lucretia Mott was born on January 3, 1793, lies about thirty miles south of Cape Cod, the easternmost peninsula of Massachusetts. The Native Americans who fished the surrounding waters called it "Faraway Island," and they introduced the first English settlers there in the mid-1600s. In 1659, Thomas Coffin's ancestor Tristram Coffin led a group of twenty Englishmen to Nantucket and was henceforth considered one of its founding fathers. After surveying this "windswept, fogbound sandbank," just 14 miles long and 3 1/2 miles wide, Coffin purchased it from the Native Americans for "30 pounds sterling and 2 beaver hats."

It was clear from the beginning that only the hardiest

men and women would survive on this rugged, desolate land. Unlike the fertile soil that was farmed on the mainland, the island's gray, sandy soil contained few of the nutrients necessary for successful cultivation. Likewise, the "relentless winds" were "hostile to planters." Scrub oak and poverty grass covered the flat, open moors, which were fit only for grazing sheep and a few cattle.

All of this mattered little to Tristram Coffin, however. Wading into the shallow waters of the sound, he had scooped up hundreds of clams, oysters, mussels, and scallops using only his bare hands. The natives had also taken him out to sea in their birch-bark canoes, where he had seen vast schools of herring, bluefish, sea bass, and cod. He had watched a pod of sperm whales, each weighing up to two tons, as they frolicked in the bay, spouting enormous geysers of water, then slapping their tails on the surface before plunging into the depths of the Atlantic. From these first observations, Tristram Coffin determined that he and the other Nantucket settlers could make a living "plowing the sea instead of the land."

Like all devout Quakers (the religious group — also known as the Society of Friends — to which the earliest settlers belonged), Coffin believed that God would provide for the needs of those who had faith. This faithfulness, combined with the hard work and thriftiness for which the Quakers were well known, allowed the new colony to prosper. The settlers' commitment to one another and to their common spirituality helped them to brave the harshness of the New England winters and to bear the isolation of island life. Their legacy was passed on to future generations, earning them a reputation for steadfastness and strength. "The strongest wind cannot stagger [their] spirit," wrote philosopher Henry David Thoreau when he visited the island.

Descendants of this original group intermarried, forming a community in which nearly everyone was related. Names such as Coffin, Folger, Starbuck, Macy, Gardiner, and Hussey were found in nearly every family tree. When Thomas Coffin Jr. married Anna Folger in 1790, they continued a long tradition of marriage between families descended from Tristram Coffin and Peter Folger, two of the earliest settlers. According to Miss Lucy Davis, a descendant from Cambridge, Massachusetts, "Grandmother [Lucretia] was in the sixth generation from Tristram Coffin and in the seventh generation from Peter Folger."

When Lucretia was born, her father was a sea captain who was well respected in the tightly knit community of whalers, fishermen, and merchants. Like most of the island's seafaring men, he was often away for months or even years at a time. Piloting his ship through dangerous waters off the coasts of New England and as far away as Africa and South America, Thomas and his crew hunted for sperm whales, which provided the colony with much-needed oil. After harpooning one of the giant mammals from smaller whaleboats, the sailors would follow it, sometimes for a hundred miles, until it tired. Often it would take several more harpoons to kill the animal, which would then be hoisted up alongside the main ship.

As this brief description suggests, whaling was a risky endeavor, and there were often fatal accidents. It was said that whalers gave up "a drop of blood for every drop of oil." Sometimes the whale would capsize one of the whaleboats or smash it into pieces with its tail. Sometimes one of the harpoon ropes would become entangled, and one or more of the crew members would be dragged into the sea.

Nonetheless, whalers faced these and other dangers because whaling, if successful, was hugely profitable. The oil extracted from the whales' blubber was used for lighting lamps and for making candles and soap. Ambergris, a natural secretion of the whales, was used to make perfume. Whale bones were used for ladies' corsets and dress hoops.

During the men's extended absences, which became an accepted part of life on Nantucket, the women and children depended upon each other for support and companionship. Each family experienced births, deaths, and other significant events within the context of the larger community. When the men returned, they were expected to fit into the social pattern established by the women in their absence. This system included community child care, task sharing, common worship, and frequent visiting between households.

"Visiting" was an important part of Nantucket tradition. Welcoming visitors into the home, offering them warm mugs of mullein tea and fresh blueberry pudding, exchanging news, and indulging in friendly conversation were among the rituals associated with the activity. Frequent visiting assured that no one family or individual became isolated and that all shared a concern for one another and the common good of the community. As biographer Dorothy Sterling explains, Lucretia learned the basics of good hospitality at a very young age:

> In the late afternoon when housework was done and visitors knocked at the door, Lucretia and Sarah raced each other for the privilege of letting them in. Long before she could see over the tops of the ladder-backed chairs, Lucretia liked to push them toward the parlor fire and urge the company to sit down. The chairs had to be arranged just right, in a sociable half-circle around the hearth. Then she would squeeze alongside Sarah on the [bench] and listen to the grownups' chatter.

Soon after Lucretia's birth, neighbors brought large containers of fish chowder, loaves of hot corn bread, and freshly baked blackberry pies. Anna's sister Phebe Hussey and her children, who lived down the street, visited daily. They played with Sarah, prepared meals, and helped with the household chores. Lucretia's Aunt

Elizabeth and Aunt Barker arrived to present the baby with hand-sewn booties and blankets. Friends stopped by to congratulate the family and to offer support during Anna's recovery.

Like most hearty Nantucket women, Anna Coffin recovered quickly. Within a week of Lucretia's birth, she was gathering firewood, shaking out the handmade rugs, and dusting the pinewood paneling in her home. It was a busy time, because Thomas was preparing for his next voyage on the whaling ship *Hepzibah*. He would be gone for at least several months, perhaps longer.

Lucretia was less than one month old when her mother bundled her up and took her down to the wharves to see Thomas off. This was to be a familiar pattern throughout Lucretia's childhood. When Lucretia was older, these partings were unpleasant for her. Despite her mother's continued reassurances that her father was an expert at sea, Lucretia remembers "the lurking fear that he would never return." And because her father was so often gone, she was left with an impression of him as "a shadowy figure, loved and respected, but never really close."

Her mother, on the other hand, was to have a profound effect on Lucretia's life. Lucretia developed "a deep love of her mother, and an indentification that lasted a lifetime." Even in her mature years, Lucretia regularly "turned to her for advice and support . . . [and] the warmth of this relationship was a source of her strength."

Like the other Nantucket women, Anna Coffin was hardworking, thrifty, and self-sufficient. She ran the affairs of the household with calm efficiency, disciplining her children in a firm but gentle manner. Besides Lucretia and Sarah, she had four more children over the years — Elizabeth, called "Eliza," in 1794, Thomas in 1798, Mary in 1800, and Martha in 1806. (Lydia, who was born in 1804, died in infancy.) With six children and a husband who was gone much of the time, Anna relied on her skillful ways of organizing their home and delegating chores.

As soon as Lucretia and her siblings were old enough to walk, they became responsible for simple household tasks. The older ones ran errands in town, gathered wood for cooking, brought in water from the well, and watched over their younger siblings. Washing, dusting, sewing, mending, and cooking also became part of their repertoire of chores, just as they had been for Anna when she was a child.

Lucretia enjoyed the more active tasks associated with housekeeping, but the sedentary ones were more of a challenge. Energetic and passionate by nature, she grew bored and restless when sitting still to mend socks, sew quilts, or peel potatoes. To distract herself, she liked to hum or sing quietly as she worked. Although Quakers generally disapproved of singing, Anna Coffin tolerated Lucretia's musical attempts and even teased her affectionately: "If thou was as far out of town as thou is out of tune, thou wouldn't get home tonight!"

17

Anna Coffin's industry extended to business: she decided to help support the family when her husband was away at sea. In the new, larger house the family moved to in 1797, she converted the front parlor into a "Shop of Goods," stocking it with cloth, groceries, hardware, and other household necessities that were not produced on the island. To replenish her inventory, she made frequent trips to the mainland, leaving Lucretia in charge of both the house and the store (though she had the help of grandmothers and aunts). Participating in business affairs and contributing to the family's income gave Lucretia a sense of independence, and she took great pride in the fact that her mother, like other Nantucket businesswomen, held a place in the larger world: "I can remember," Lucretia wrote, "how our mothers were employed while our fathers were at sea. At that time it required some money and some courage to get to Boston. They were obliged to go to that city, make their trades, exchange their oils and candles for dry goods, set their own price, keep their own accounts."

Throughout her childhood, Lucretia observed that women were as well suited to the public sphere of business and enterprise as they were to the private sphere of home and family. It was a lesson she remembered well, one that would later serve to strengthen her belief in gender equality and to motivate her activities on behalf of women's rights.

Because her older sister Sarah was handicapped,

Lucretia assumed the role of the eldest child. Sarah's handicap has been established through family documents (which are few), but the exact nature of her disability — whether mental, physical, or both — is not known. In the nineteenth century, disabilities of any sort were often feared and misunderstood. Apparently the Coffins rarely discussed Sarah's affliction even among themselves. Like most other families in this situation, they preferred not to draw attention to the matter, accepting it as God's will and proceeding quietly with their own lives.

Fortunately, Lucretia was well suited to her leadership role. Though physically small and slightly built, she was highly energetic, industrious, and quick to learn. When Anna placed her in charge of the household and went off to the mainland to barter for goods, Lucretia had no trouble keeping the other children busy and out of mischief. They swept the hearth, scrubbed the iron cooking pots, polished windows, stacked wood, drew fresh water from the well, peeled potatoes for dinner, and picked wild blackberries for dessert. When Anna would return from her mainland journey, she would praise Lucretia's competence: "Thou [hast done] well, Lucretia," she would say, tenderly smoothing the dark hair around Lucretia's blushing face.

Though she was always kind and fair, Lucretia seemed to revel in her authority. She was quick to reprimand someone who wasn't pulling his or her own weight in the household, dawdled over a simple task,

19

or completed a job in a slipshod manner. She also tended to lecture her younger siblings on their behavior and answered back when she was criticized by older relatives. Her mother tried to temper Lucretia's impatience: "Thy sister will learn, Long Tongue," she reminded her when she corrected Eliza's early spelling mistakes. "Thou must give her more time."

But time was something Lucretia felt she never had enough of. She had a quick mind, asked questions constantly, and was always ready for adventure. Once, when still a toddler, she wandered into town and was several blocks from home before her aunt discovered she was missing. Her mother sent her to her room as punishment, but "Lucretia's gray eyes grew black with anger" and "she stamped her tiny feet" and refused to go.

In her Nantucket grammar school, Lucretia was a fast learner. She frequently completed her "sums" (arithmetic) and "copy work" (writing practice) before her classmates, and then was forced to sit quietly with her hands folded while they finished. Although she tried to be patient, "boredom often put an end to her good resolutions. . . . She groaned out loud or imitated [her cousin] Mary under her breath until the girls sitting nearby were convulsed with giggles." This behavior often landed little Lucretia on the "repentance stool," where "she spent more time . . . than she cared to tell her mother about."

When she was not in school or at home doing

chores, Lucretia liked to visit the harborfront. It was here that the many businesses relating to the whaling industry thrived: candle factories, sail shops, black-smith shops, cordage (rope) stores, and cooperages (for barrel-making) lined the streets near the wharves and bustled with activity. It was here too that Lucretia, often accompanied by Eliza, could "glimpse the wide world beyond Nantucket Sound. . . . Olive-skinned workmen with gold rings through their ears who spoke Portuguese . . . sailors . . . Indians [who were] descendants of the original natives of Nantucket . . . Negroes whose fathers had been brought from Africa on slave ships."

In the evenings, the Coffins gathered near the fire to recite Bible verses and tell stories. Rocking her brother Thomas in the cradle, Lucretia listened intently to every detail of her mother's excursions to Boston and, when her father was home, to his tales of whaling adventures. She imagined what other Massachusetts towns and their inhabitants might look like, and the thrill of being out on the open sea. She promised herself that someday she too would leave the island to have adventures of her own.

In the meantime, however, Lucretia's day-to-day life was defined by her parents' affiliation with the Society of Friends. The Society had originated in England in the mid-seventeenth century under the leadership of a young preacher named George Fox. Friends or "Quakers" (the name given them by English Protestants who observed them "trembling at the word of the Lord") were considered radicals by the Church of England. They rejected most of the philosophies and practices of the established churches and "sought to live the lives of early Christians." They refused to attend established church services, to hire ministers, to pay church tithes and government taxes, and to support or fight in wars. They believed that men and women of all races were equal in the sight of God. (To show this, they addressed one another by using "thee" and "thou" instead of the more informal pronoun "you.") In addition, they refused to take oaths of any kind, believing that honesty should not be reserved for occasions such as trials and business transactions but should be a condition of daily living.

As a result of their beliefs, the Friends in England were "whipped, jailed, and even executed." This widespread persecution forced them to emigrate to America in the seventeenth century, where they attempted to establish themselves in the Colonies. But here too there were incidents of persecution, for "Puritan New England reacted violently to the Friends' preaching." Gradually, however, they won converts, expanded their families, and settled peacefully in communities from New York to the Carolinas.

Fifty years after the first Quaker settlers established themselves on Nantucket, their descendants constructed a meetinghouse on Main Street. The building itself was "a bare, undecorated room, cold in Winter, hot and airless in Summer. Its whitewashed benches were hard [and] their straight backs offered little comfort." This lack of adornment reflected the Quaker values of thriftiness and simplicity; Friends believed that emphasis on material goods distracted people from their spiritual lives. They also believed in living simply and dressing plainly.

Twice each week, on "First Days" (Sundays) and again on "Fifth Days" (Thursdays), Lucretia attended Meeting (the Quaker equivalent of a worship service) with her family. Seated on opposite sides of the room, the men and women meditated silently, opening their hearts to divine inspiration. When someone "felt a concern to speak," he or she would rise and share an idea, recite a Bible verse, or pose a question to the others. The elders, who were chosen for their ability to articulate divinely inspired messages, sat on a separate bench in front, facing the group. Both men and women were designated as elders, for the Friends believed in spiritual and intellectual equality.

Like all Quakers, the Nantucket Friends believed that every person, regardless of race, social standing, nationality, or knowledge of religion, possessed an "Inner Light," which was "the true light, which lighteth every man that cometh into the world" (John 1:9). This was the cornerstone of Quaker philosophy, which led them to "deny the special authority of an ordained clergy and insist instead on the priesthood of all believers." Although they frequently read and quoted from the Bible, Friends regarded the Inward Christ (a person's Inner Light or soul) as the highest moral authority.

Unlike Puritan churches of the nineteenth century, which emphasized the inherent wickedness of the soul and the possibility of eternal damnation, Quakers emphasized humans' capacity for love and compassion. Lucretia and her siblings were therefore introduced to "a God of love and hope rather than a God of wrath" and a religion that emphasized "the here-and-now rather than the hereafter."

The Quaker life was designed to be a simple one, free from the distractions that might interfere with one's connection to the Inner Light. It was a life that required sacrifice and discipline, concepts that the young and spirited Lucretia sometimes found difficult to apply to her own life. Occasionally, she rebelled against the Friends' strict code of behavior and dress. She would squirm impatiently during silent meeting, whisper secrets to her sister Eliza, and wear shoes with bright blue bows to contrast with her plain gray dress. At family gatherings, she would entertain the younger children by mimicking the elders. Standing before them, she would lower her voice and make a solemn face: "Are Friends careful to live within the bounds of their circumstances?" she would ask as the children broke into delighted laughter.

As Lucretia grew older, however, she developed a deep respect for Quaker ways and beliefs. She admired her ancestors for enduring persecution so that they might attain religious freedom for themselves and for future generations.

One of the things that made a deep impression on Lucretia was hearing a traveling woman minister, Elizabeth Coggeshall, speak at the local meetinghouse. The men and women who were able to travel and preach on behalf of the Society were called Public Friends. Coggeshall had even traveled to England. According to biographer Margaret Hope Bacon, "Lucretia stood in awe of her. To be a Public Friend, to travel and be listened to, to what higher calling could a Quaker girl aspire?" Lucretia couldn't know it at the time, but someday she would follow in Coggeshall's footsteps.

The island life of Nantucket and the ways of Quakerism combined to provide Lucretia with a childhood environment of equality, safety, and peace. In Lucretia's mind, these qualities would always be interrelated. Over the course of her adult life, and with varying degrees of success, she would seek to recreate this environment, both for herself and for others. Eventually she would leave her island home and make her place in the larger world. Yet in her heart she would always remain a true daughter of Nantucket.

CHAPTER 3

Equal Minds, Open Hearts

Early in the morning on a crisp winter's day in 1803, the town crier announced the entrance of a ship into Nantucket Harbor. Lucretia and Eliza, busy with their chores in the kitchen, looked up briefly, shrugged, and quickly returned to work. It had been three years since their father had left on a whaling expedition to the South Atlantic, and they had long since given up running to the "captain's walk" (a small rooftop porch) to scan the horizon for his new vessel, the *Tryal*.

There had been no letters, no special messages, in fact no word at all concerning the fate of the *Tryal*, its captain, or its crew. Anna Coffin and her children had waited patiently. They had stood at the dock and watched other Nantucket ships return safely, their crews happily reunited with family and friends.

Throughout the first year of her husband's absence, Anna Coffin had remained optimistic. The fate of the *Tryal* lay in God's hands, and she believed that he would not disappoint them. Lucretia remembered that her mother would stand before the fireplace on dark winter evenings and read aloud from the Scriptures: "Don't be impatient. Wait for the Lord . . . wait, and He will help you" (Psalm 27:14). When news reached Nantucket that Uriah Hussey (Lucretia's uncle) and his ship had been lost at sea, Anna's faith did not waver.

But when two years passed, then three, and there was still no word from Thomas, doubt crept slowly into Anna's heart. Her usual cheerfulness was overshadowed by anxiety, and her once-frequent smile all but disappeared.

Lucretia sensed her mother's concern and tried to ease the burden of her single parenthood. She prayed daily for the strength to curb her naturally quick temper and did more than her share of the housework. "Lucretia [was] trained to regard good housekeeping with wholesome respect," writes biographer Otelia Cromwell. "Such expertness did Lucretia achieve in the performance of the numberless duties involved in the daily routine that she reflected all through her life the results of her early apprenticeship." She gathered wood, swept and polished the floors, and rocked the babies until her arms ached. She taught the older children their letters and how to make rugs by sewing together scraps of brightly colored material.

Anna used the extra time that Lucretia's assistance gave her to look after her shop; the profits from it were now the only income she had to support her family.

She was grateful for her daughter's help and was careful to express her appreciation: "Thou does good work, Lucretia," she would say. Her sentiments were echoed by visiting aunts, cousins, and grandmothers, who commented on Lucretia's "early maturity" and her skillful handling of the younger children.

Lucretia enjoyed their approval, but she would have gladly traded their compliments for just one glimpse of her father. Despite her frequent efforts to recall his voice, his face, his walk, and the feel of his hands, the memory of him grew hopelessly dimmer with each passing day.

But later that winter's morning in 1803, Lucretia found herself at the front door, standing face to face with a tall, thin, and "deeply suntanned" sailor whom she faintly recognized as her father. Her startled shout brought her mother and the rest of the children running quickly in from the yard. Discarding the Quaker custom of restrained affection, they promptly smothered Thomas with hugs and kisses. "The rejoicing in the big back kitchen that morning was something none of [them] ever forgot," writes biographer Margaret Hope Bacon.

Standing back to admire his family, Thomas marveled at the changes that had occurred during his absence. Young Thomas, whom he remembered as a chubby toddler, was now a lanky five-year-old boy. Baby Mary, born just a few months before his departure, was now a feisty three-year-old. But it was the difference in

Lucretia that impressed Thomas the most. Surely this poised young lady was not the same awkward seven-year-old who had waved good-bye to him from the docks! Dark-haired, hazel-eyed, and petite, she had "an amused smile that lurked at the corners of her mouth." As Thomas watched her "laughing and chattering" with her sister Eliza, he noticed that she seemed to be "lit by an inner fire" and "seemed [much] inclined to talk."

That evening, the family gathered before the fireplace to listen to tales of their father's adventures. Shortly after reaching the coast of South America, he told them, the *Tryal* had been captured by the Spanish fleet. The fleet's officers accused Thomas of fishing illegally in their waters and took him to Valparaiso, Chile, to be judged by the Spanish court. While awaiting his trial, he stayed with a kind family who taught him the Spanish language and customs. (Years later, Lucretia remembered her father saying "Gracias" and "Buenos Dias" to surprised Nantucket neighbors.) He had written a few letters home, but they had never reached Nantucket.

As the weeks and months passed, Thomas's case remained unresolved. Frustrated by the court's delay, he asked if he could be released (his crew had already been freed) if he relinquished the *Tryal* to the Spaniards. They agreed, and Thomas set out on foot across South America, intending to somehow make his way home.

He headed north toward the towering Andes Mountains, risking hunger, heat, and cold in hopes of making it safely to the more friendly harbors of Brazil. During his journey, which lasted a few months, he covered hundreds of miles. Finally he reached an eastern port, where he convinced the captain of an American ship to take him back home.

The details of this impressive story stayed with Lucretia for the rest of her life. Her family had endured a long and difficult time, but their steadfast faith, determination, and resourcefulness had seen them through. That week she entered the Main Street Meetinghouse with a renewed sense of hope and purpose. In silence she prayed that she, like her parents, would remain faithful and courageous in times of danger and doubt. "Trials . . . are not without their purpose," she later wrote.

For the next several weeks, all was peaceful in the Coffin household. But Lucretia's delight over her father's safe return was soon replaced by apprehension. In the course of his long journey, Thomas had promised himself that if he returned home safely, he would give up the seafaring life. One evening, after a delicious dinner of codfish and stewed cranberries, he announced his intention to move the family to Boston and become a merchant.

For Lucretia, who had spent her entire childhood on Nantucket, leaving the island would be "a wrenching break." For the next several nights she lay awake in bed, trying to sort out her feelings. She had often wondered what life on the mainland was like, but now that the opportunity to find out had truly arrived, she realized that she had mixed emotions. Part of her longed for the adventure of living in a big city, but at the same time her heart ached at the thought of leaving her beloved island home. The salty sea air, windswept moors, and long, narrow beaches were part of her earliest and most precious memories. She made a silent vow to keep those memories alive and to return someday, perhaps with a family of her own. "Lucretia took her Nantucket in serious affection," observes Otelia Cromwell, "[and later] continued to recall [her] days on the island. . . . Indeed the mere mention of Nantucket awakened in her a nostalgia of mingled emotions . . . [for] it was her belief that social relations and happy times were more enduring in Nantucket than elsewhere."

Lucretia's mother was also "deeply rooted" on Nantucket and struggled with her own mixed feelings about leaving. In the end, however, she supported her husband's wish to work at a less risky occupation.

In keeping with Quaker tradition, the Coffins lived simply and had few material possessions that were not of some practical use. Yet there was still plenty to be done in preparation for the move. With Lucretia's help, Anna packed the "thousand and one things that [had to] be taken along" into wooden barrels and boxes. Lucretia also helped her mother close the shop, and she took care of the other children while her parents signed the papers that transferred ownership of their house to Lucretia's widowed Aunt Phebe.

In July of 1804, the Coffins bid a fond farewell to

their neighbors and relatives and boarded the packet ship for Boston. Lucretia stood at the rail and pulled her bonnet tightly around her face. Eliza stood with her, and together they watched until "there was nothing left of Nantucket but a lone seagull silhouetted against the sky."

After they arrived in Boston, the Coffins settled into a house on Green Street, located in a residential district of the city. The neighborhood was crisscrossed by quiet side streets and held a commanding view of Boston Harbor.

Each morning when she awoke, Lucretia pressed her nose against the glass windowpane of her bedroom and watched the ever-expanding city of thirty thousand come to life. Horses pulling fine carriages clip-clopped their way along the cobblestones, carrying gentleman passengers to the countinghouses (business offices) on the waterfront. Pedestrians on their way to work in shops and factories scurried like so many ants up and down the narrow alleyways. The masts of tall ships in the harbor cast their long morning shadows across the glistening water. As Lucretia surveyed the scene from her second-story perch, the smell of her mother's blueberry pudding drifted up from the kitchen. Perhaps life in Boston would not be so bad after all, she thought.

As had been their habit on Nantucket, the Coffin children rose early, ate a hearty breakfast, and did their chores. When they were finished, Anna took the younger children for a walk while Lucretia and Eliza ran down to the harbor. When they reached the waterfront, the two sisters stood shoulder to shoulder on the wharves, watching in deep fascination as burly, suntanned sailors loaded goods from the colonies onto huge sailing ships bound for Europe and the Far East. At the same time, English, Portuguese, and Caribbean sailors were unloading the goods from their own tallmasted ships — tea, china, rugs, and bananas — for trade in Boston. The familiar smell of the salt air and the sound of the ships' bells were comforting to the island-bred children, who were now part of a much larger, faster-paced world.

After school, the girls liked to visit their father's office on the waterfront. As they approached, Lucretia read the wooden sign above the door: "Coffin & Sumner — Merchants of General Goods," it said. Here, in one of the dozens of countinghouses that faced the harbor, Thomas and his partner Jesse Sumner sold candles, sugar, flour, oils, cotton, wool, and other necessities. The store was much larger and far busier than their Nantucket "Shop of Goods" had ever been, but even a short visit kindled fond memories for Lucretia.

Boston was growing rapidly, and Thomas Coffin's business flourished. In 1806, the Coffins moved to a larger home on Round Lane, which they had purchased for $5,600.00. By early nineteenth-century standards, this was considered "an enormous sum of money to pay for a house." At first, Lucretia's parents were somewhat

33

troubled by their prosperity, for they had been used to the struggles and hardships of island life. Furthermore, the Quaker values of thriftiness and simplicity were difficult to reconcile with their newly acquired wealth. But they soon realized that they would need the profits from Thomas's business to properly educate their children.

During their first two years in Boston, the Coffins enrolled their children in a private school, but they soon transferred them to public school. Although they could afford to send their children to a private school, Anna and Thomas preferred the more "democratic" atmosphere of public schools, where their children could "mingle with all classes without distinction." This taught Lucretia a valuable lesson that deeply affected her thoughts on human equality: "It was the custom then," she wrote, "to send the children of such families [as ours] to select schools; but my parents feared that would minister to a feeling of class pride, which they felt was sinful to cultivate in [us]. And this I am glad to remember, because it gave me a feeling of sympathy for the patient and struggling poor, which, but for this experience, I might never have known."

It was while she was attending the Boston public schools that Lucretia first became aware of the gender bias that existed in education. Girls, she discovered, went to school just six months of the year, while boys attended year-round. A girl's education ended abruptly after eighth grade, but boys were encouraged to continue. "Many nineteenth-century families believed that girls should be educated only for careers as wives and mothers," explains biographer Gerald Kurland. "[They] did not feel that girls needed or could profit from a formal, academic education. It was far better, they felt, to teach them how to sew, cook, and clean, and care for a husband and children." The advice of one Boston resident concerning his daughter's education appeared in that city's evening newspaper around this time. It is typical of the nineteenth-century view on "a woman's proper place":

> Teach her what's useful, how to shun deluding;
> To roast, to toast, to boil and mix a pudding;
> To knit, to spin, to sew, to make or mend;
> To scrub, to rub, to earn and not to spend.

Fortunately for Lucretia, her parents did not believe in such gender prejudice. On Nantucket, boys and girls had received an equal education. If the Boston public schools could not provide that for their children, Anna and Thomas decided, then they must find a private school that would.

Nine Partners Boarding School near Poughkeepsie, New York, was the answer to their dilemma. Founded in 1796 by nine Quaker gentlemen, this co-educational school "embodied the most progressive educational principles . . . and combined Quaker religious tradition with the most up-to-date academic disciplines."

Lucretia was thirteen and Eliza twelve when they set out via the Mail Stage for New York's Hudson River Valley. The journey, which consisted of three days of bouncing over dusty roads, "was a little like setting out to sea," Lucretia later recalled. She liked the independence of traveling without her parents and found herself looking forward to new adventures at school.

Timid Eliza, however, was more fearful about leaving home. Lucretia attempted to distract her from her negative feelings by keeping her busy. During stops for food and lodging, the girls unpacked and rechecked the items that the school had requested they bring:

1 or 2 plain bonnets
1 cloak (not silk)
2 gingham gowns suitable for the season
2 or 3 nightcaps
3 or 4 long check aprons
1 pair of scissors & a paper of pins

"If the clothing sent [is] not plain or requires much washing, it is to be returned," the school's letter had warned, "at the PARENTS' expense."

Upon their arrival, the Coffin sisters received a warm welcome from the school's staff. A teacher gave them a tour of the three-story, barnlike building that provided "comfortable if austere" living space for the students. Lucretia was quick to notice the two main entrances: one for boys and one for girls. To her amazement, there was even a high fence separating the girls' play-ground from that of the boys. Girls and boys received an equal education, the teacher, explained, but they attended separate classes and were housed in separate dormitories.

The first weeks passed uneventfully. Like the other girls, Lucretia and Eliza gradually learned the behaviors that the school required. These included "walking to Meeting in an orderly and becoming manner," keeping their belongings "in good order and repair," and main-taining a "commendable decorum" during class.

Grateful for the privilege of attending Nine Partners, Lucretia came to view the school's segregation policy as a minor inconvenience. She soon learned that, despite their physical separation, males and females managed to communicate. Messages were sent through relatives on either side who "were permitted to speak under suitable inspection and at proper seasons."

One such message was passed along to the girls' side just a few weeks after Lucretia and Eliza had arrived. It seems that one of the younger boys had been placed in a room by himself and denied supper as punishment for a minor transgression. Lucretia felt that the sentence was too severe, and she persuaded "meek and terrified" Eliza to help her smuggle food to him. Using a secret passageway, they arrived on the "forbidden side of the house," slipped the offender several pieces of buttered bread, and returned to their dormitory unnoticed.

This incident was significant in Lucretia's development as a free thinker. By undermining the school's decision to punish her classmate, she established a precedent for overcoming challenges to do what she thought was right, a principle she would embrace throughout her lifetime. Although she did not break rules arbitrarily, she believed in standing up for truth and justice, no matter what the consequences. If those consequences included ridicule, punishment, or even physical harm, she accepted them without complaint.

Opportunities for such risks were few, however, in the day-to-day lives of the Nine Partners students. They rose early, dressed, ate a simple breakfast, and then filed in an orderly fashion to their classrooms. Lucretia and Eliza were enrolled in Beginning Studies, which included "Reading, Writing, and Accounts, together with English Grammar," "Branches of Mathematics," and "Business and Domestic Employment." The following year, philosophy, history, religion, and social studies were added to the girls' curriculum.

The classes at Nine Partners broadened Lucretia's horizons and challenged her intellect. She excelled in all of her subjects and was accepted into an advanced literature course. This course became Lucretia's favorite, her love of words and her outgoing personality predisposing her to a flair for poetry and rhyme. She read widely in works by poets and writers such as William Shakespeare, John Milton, William Wordsworth, and Samuel Taylor Coleridge. "Lucretia could barely carry a tune, [but] she had an unfailing sense of rhythm and an acute musical ear," writes Otelia Cromwell. "She treasured lines of didactic [morally instructive] poetry from the . . . poets of the 18th century whose humanitarian moods struck a responsive chord in her soul."

Her favorite was a poem by the English writer William Cowper (1731-1800) entitled *The Task*. Years later, her children recalled her "repeat[ing] page after page [of it] as the family sat together on the porch . . . in the dusky summer evenings":

Scenes must be beautiful, which, daily viewed,
Please daily, and whose novelty survives
Long knowledge and scrutiny of years —

Nor rural sights alone, but rural sounds
Exhilarate the spirit and restore
The tone of languid Nature.

Nature inanimate employs sweet sounds,
But animated nature sweeter still,
To soothe and satisfy the human ear.

Activities outside the classroom included twice-weekly Meetings, frequent hikes, and occasional tea parties (co-educational but closely supervised). In addition to these school-sponsored events, the students created their own amusements. Lucretia and her friends especially enjoyed "playing Meeting." This game consisted of a mock hearing, during which one student played the "offender" and was brought before the others, who acted as "elders." A full report was then given to "the Meeting," and punishment, if necessary, was pronounced. Lucretia delighted in this game, for she was often called upon to be the presiding elder. "Friends," she would declare in the most solemn voice she could muster, "we have visited Tabitha Field — and — we labored with her — and we — think — we — MELLOWED her some."

Guest speakers, chosen by the school's board of directors, made frequent appearances and provided another form of instructional entertainment. A co-founder of the school named Elias Hicks was one of the speakers. Hicks was a preacher with a small but steadily increasing band of followers who were attracted to his "old school" philosophy. Like the early Quakers, he believed "in the direct relationship between God and conscience," rejecting the need for hired ministers, strict religious dogma, and traditional sacraments. He was called an extremist in other parts of the country, but the community at Nine Partners was sympathetic to his ideas.

Hicks was an inspirational speaker, a "tall and gaunt" man "with a beaked nose and piercing eyes." His mission at Nine Partners was to convince both students and staff of the injustice of slavery. "[I must] shake [my] beloved Society of Friends awake to [abolish] slavery," he told his audience. His accounts of the harsh treatment of blacks brought to the United States from Africa made a deep impression on young Lucretia, who became angry as she listened to his stories.

Hicks's personal plea for abolition (stopping the slave trade and freeing those who were slaves) compelled Lucretia to educate herself further about "this wrong crying to be righted." She obtained a copy of Thomas Clarkson's *Essay on Slavery,* in which the prominent English abolitionist gave disturbing accounts of how slaves were mistreated on the ships that transported them. According to Margaret Hope Bacon, he detailed "the sexual abuse of the women, the torture of defiant slaves, the human cargoes thrown overboard in order to earn insurance money." These horrors enraged Lucretia. Her innate "gift of empathy" allowed her to "easily put herself in the place of another and feel his or her pain or joy."

Besides attending Hicks's lectures and doing additional reading, Lucretia attended lectures on abolition given by the school's director, James Mott Sr. Like Hicks, Mott was an abolitionist who believed that Quakers should play an active role in social reform. Years later, Lucretia recalled that Mott's philosophy "helped determine the course [my] life would take."

CHAPTER 4

City of Brotherly Love

During daily recess at Nine Partners, Lucretia sometimes managed to "catch a glimpse" of Mott's grandson, James Mott Jr., and was immediately attracted to him. James Jr., who was five years older than Lucretia, was a teacher at the school. He was "the tallest boy in the school with blue eyes and a shock of sandy hair." His sister Sarah, Lucretia's best friend, described him as "gentle and soft-spoken." When Sarah invited Lucretia to spend a vacation with the Mott family in Mamaroneck, New York, Lucretia gladly accepted.

Though naturally shy, James was interested in getting to know Lucretia better. With Sarah along to chaperone, he took Lucretia for walks along the shore of Long Island Sound. They sipped lemonade in the shade beside the family's flour mill and went sailing on the nearby pond. James was "bashful" and "too shy to talk much," but Lucretia — who was never at a loss for words — talked enough for both of them.

As she told him about her island home, her move to Boston, her family, and her friends at school, James listened attentively. He seemed content to let her steer the conversation, and she was comforted by his quiet, gentle presence. "They were in many ways opposites," writes biographer Margaret Hope Bacon. "He was tall and blond, she was short and dark. He was taciturn and serious; she was talkative and merry. . . . He was cautious; she was impetuous and sometimes gullible. [But] they both seemed to delight in these differences." Their relationship blossomed. By the end of her two-week visit, Lucretia knew that she could easily spend the rest of her life with young James Mott.

When she returned to school, Lucretia applied herself to her work even more diligently. By 1808, when she was only fifteen, she had finished all the courses the school offered. Despite her young age, the board of directors offered Lucretia a teaching position. School records show that "at the end of two years at Nine Partners, [she] was regarded as the best student among the advanced girls in the academy, and . . . was [not] outdistanced by any of the boys. . . . [She was therefore] made assistant teacher to Deborah Rogers who taught 'Reading, Grammar and Arithmetik.'" Before Lucretia began the job, however, she wanted to go home; she hadn't seen her family for two years.

By the time she returned from Boston, the school had undergone certain changes. For one thing, James Mott Sr. was no longer superintendent; for another, several additional teaching assistants had been hired. Lucretia had known that she would receive only room and board in exchange for her teaching services. But she became angry when she discovered that Ms. Rogers, "a mature, experienced, and highly competent teacher," received less than half of the salary paid to the much younger and less experienced James Mott Jr. The inequity troubled her, for she had been taught that women were intellectually as well as spiritually equal to men. The discrepancy in salaries directly contradicted this belief. "It did not take her long to conclude," biographer Gerald Kurland has observed, "that the economic discrimination suffered by women was based exclusively upon their sex and not upon any talent or lack of ability."

Lucretia's first encounter with gender discrimination, like her first encounter with the slavery issue, made a lasting impression. "The injustice of this distinction was so apparent that I early resolved to claim for myself all that an impartial Creator had bestowed," she wrote. But because she was the newest and youngest member of the school staff, Lucretia did not reveal her true feelings immediately. Clearly, she told herself, this was an injustice that would take more to rectify than simply sliding bread under a door to a hungry classmate!

And so, for the time being, she accepted the terms of her position and remained at Nine Partners for another year. Teaching left her little free time, but what time she had she spent with young James Mott. As their fondness for one another grew, James expressed his own thoughts and feelings more frequently. He confessed that he didn't enjoy teaching but felt obligated to continue at the school to help support his parents.

Lucretia had guessed this already, having found him to be someone who "took serious views of life, and was much given to religious contemplation." He was sometimes gloomy too, whereas she was typically hopeful. But the two of them seemed to be drawn closer by their differences. She was becoming deeply attached to James, and he returned her affections. Absorbed in their work and wrapped in the warm glow of romance, they remained, for a time, blissfully unaware of political events that would directly affect their future.

For this — the first decade of the nineteenth century — was an unsettled time for the United States. The Revolutionary War had been won more than twenty years earlier, yet America continued to struggle over its differences with Great Britain. Tensions were mounting between the two countries, and would culminate in the War of 1812. In Europe, French General Napoleon Bonaparte was marching his troops eastward, winning numerous battles and claiming more and more of the continent for France.

President Thomas Jefferson, who was serving his second term in office, had declared a trade embargo against both Britain and France. Though necessary as a peace measure, the embargo had a depressing effect on American businesses. Economic ties with Europe were essentially cut off, which greatly reduced American imports and exports, and forced the United States to produce many of the goods that it had formerly purchased from the Europeans.

Back home in Boston, Thomas Coffin found himself at a crossroads as a result of these political events. With waterfront trade in Boston nearly at a standstill, he decided, in 1809, to move the family to Philadelphia. There, about twenty miles outside the city in French Creek, he invested in a nail factory owned by several of his cousins.

Meanwhile, Lucretia was nearing the end of her year's commitment at Nine Partners. Because her father was doing well in business, he had asked her to come home; she didn't need to work to support herself or the family. When Lucretia told James that she would be going to Philadelphia, he said, "I shall miss thee, Lucretia." Understandably, Lucretia felt torn. Parting with James, even briefly, would be difficult. But three years had passed since she had spent any significant time with her family, and she longed to be with them again.

The day arrived when Lucretia bid farewell to Nine Partners. After a few days' travel by stage through New York and New Jersey, she boarded the ferry at Camden for the short ride across the Delaware River. Standing at the boat's rail, she studied the shoreline ahead, wondering what was in store for her on the opposite side. Would she feel at home in this new place? What would it be like to be with her family again?

A warm welcome awaited her in Philadelphia. Her family was gathered at the dock, chattering nervously as they awaited Lucretia's homecoming. When the boat arrived, they saw "a trim figure in dove gray with bonnet and cap hiding her long brown hair . . . chin firm . . . forehead high . . . fine dark eyes bright and knowing . . . strid[ing] across the gangplank with a clatter of heel and toe that announced strength and determination." How different she appeared, her parents remarked, from "the little girl who had waved good-bye in Boston."

The family's new residence on South Second Street was a short carriage ride away. It was a stately red-brick dwelling brightened by white wood trim, large windows, and polished marble steps. Lucretia noticed that her mother had managed to arrange the furnishings inside in a comfortable fashion so that, despite the interior's formal character, visitors would feel immediately at home.

After the family enjoyed a hearty meal, Lucretia's brother Thomas offered her a carriage tour of the city. As they bounced over the cobblestones in the family's much-used buggy, Lucretia noticed familiar New England names such as "Folger," "Hussey," "Wright," and "Mayhew" beside the doorways of nearby homes and businesses. "More of us here than in Boston," Thomas reminded her, referring to the city's Quaker population. It had not taken the Coffins long to fit in.

As they rolled along the tree-lined streets and traveled around fountain-filled squares, Lucretia tried to recall what she knew of the city's history. At school she had learned that the English Quaker William Penn had founded Philadelphia in 1681. That year King Charles II had given Penn permission to create a "Holy Experiment" — an American colony where both political and religious freedom would be enjoyed by all. The king, it seems, owed Penn's father a large sum of money, and when Penn proposed that the debt be paid by granting him land in the Colonies, the king quickly agreed.

Named for its founder, Pennsylvania became, in the nineteenth century, a place where the concepts of democracy and human rights were fully tested. As its capital and largest commercial center, Philadelphia (known as "the City of Brotherly Love") was a progressive, attractive city that reflected Penn's democratic philosophy. Many of its wide, shady streets had names such as "Mulberry," "Pine," "Walnut," "Cherry," and "Spruce." Neighborhoods were designed "with a geometrical precision" and flowed easily from one to another. Public squares were abundant, and marketplaces were readily accessible by foot or by carriage. The city's waterworks — the first of their kind in the United States — used steam power to force water from the nearby Schuylkill River through wooden "pipes" and into homes and businesses. Benjamin Franklin, a distant relative of the Coffins, had greatly influenced the city's modern character: he had established several of its first scientific, educational, and public-service facilities.

Unlike Boston, whose conservative Puritan majority held a strong prejudice against the more liberal Quakers, Philadelphia was a sanctuary for the Friends. They were organized into large groups (called "Monthly Meetings")* on the basis of where they lived. Since Lucretia's family lived on the south end of Second Street, near Walnut, they attended the Southern District Monthly Meeting; the family name was formally entered in the records there in February 1809.

Lucretia was glad to be home, and when she first arrived in Philadelphia, she didn't have much time to think about James Mott. But after she was settled in, she was periodically restless; she had a feeling that something — or someone — was missing. She reminisced frequently about the time she and James had spent together.

One day, as she accompanied her father to his factory in French Creek, she was unusually quiet. Could it be that her friend James Mott was the object of her day-dreams? her father asked. That simple question prompted Lucretia to tell him everything. James was

---

*The Society of Friends was simply and logically structured. Individual Quakers belonged to Monthly Meetings, groups that worshiped together every week and met for business once a month. A regional group of Monthly Meetings made up a Quarterly Meeting, which gathered for business four times a year. And a group (also determined by geographical location) of Quarterly Meetings made up a Yearly Meeting, which gathered for business annually.

unhappy in his teaching position, she said, but felt obligated to keep it for financial reasons. She missed him terribly, but she had no wish to return to Nine Partners. Her father understood completely and proposed a solution: he would write to James and offer to employ him as a clerk at the factory.

James Mott sent a grateful letter of acceptance immediately. Lucretia was delighted at the prospect of seeing him again, and she helped her mother prepare the spare room for him. (In those days it was common for a young apprentice to reside in his employer's home.) But despite the fact that they would be living in the same house, James and Lucretia would not be permitted to spend time alone. In the nineteenth century, unmarried couples were allowed to "date" only under closely supervised conditions, and physical contact of any sort — including kissing and hugging — was strictly forbidden.

Soon after being reunited, James and Lucretia announced their intention to be married. Lucretia's parents gave their blessing, but Quaker tradition also required the approval of the Meeting. Dutifully, Lucretia and James followed the procedure stated in the Rules of Discipline:

Proposals of marriage are to be presented in writing to the preparative [committee of the] meeting of which the woman is a member, signed by the parties; . . . [then] forwarded to the monthly meeting. . . . Their said intentions should be minuted (noted) and inquiry made concerning parents or guardians. . . . Two Friends are to be appointed to inquire into the man's clearness for proceeding in marriage; . . . and [also] the woman's. . . . At the second monthly meeting, they are to present, separately, in their respective meetings, . . . and should . . . there appear to be no obstruction . . . the meeting is to leave them at liberty to accomplish their marriage according to the order of our Society.

James was nervous about the prospect of appearing before the elders, but he later wrote that he felt "calm and composed" during the actual proceedings. "[It was] as if I had been speaking before so many cabbage stumps," he told his parents. "Our appearance was plain, and becoming to the occasion. All parties were pleased with it."

On April 10, 1811, Lucretia Coffin and James Mott were married in the Pine Street Meetinghouse. Lucretia, dressed in the traditional plain gray, radiated a youthful beauty. Her long, thick brown hair was neatly tucked under her bonnet, and her eyes shone brightly with anticipation. At a signal from one of the elders, she rose gracefully from the wooden bench and repeated her vows from memory: "I, Lucretia Coffin, take thee, James Mott, to be my husband, promising with divine assistance to be unto thee a true and loving wife so long as we both shall live." James, dressed in black and sporting a new wide-brimmed hat, repeated the vow to Lucretia — and so began a union that would endure for nearly sixty years.

As was the custom in those days, the newlyweds had no honeymoon. And, since it was customary for the couple to initially live with the bride's parents, Lucretia and James shared a room in the Coffin residence for the first several months. Each day James went off to work with Thomas, and Lucretia remained behind to help Anna run the house. By August, the couple had saved enough money to rent a new, spacious home at 48 Union Street, not far from Lucretia's parents. "Rent is $300 a year," James wrote to his father. "We shall begin housekeeping (move) as soon as we can get ready. . . . Business is very dull."

Their newfound independence was short-lived, however. Orders for building materials dwindled, forcing production at the nail factory to halt. As a last resort, Thomas reduced James's salary, and since there wasn't enough revenue from the factory to support two households, the Coffins (all six of them) moved in with James and Lucretia. "Things in the mercantile line [are] very gloomy," James wrote to his parents. "Many failures have taken place, and no doubt many more will. . . . Those who have money [now] keep it in their own hands."

Lucretia also wrote to her husband's parents, announcing that she was pregnant and asking for moral support as she and James faced their first struggles: "James is 'down cellar' lately, and though he is acknowledged to be head and shoulders above his brethren, . . . he is often complaining of his littleness. . . . So if you have any [advice] for his encouragement, please produce it." In the face of these economic difficulties, Lucretia remained more optimistic than James: "The Lord will provide," she reminded him.

On August 3, 1812, Lucretia gave birth to a daughter, whom she named Anna. In those times it was the custom for a woman to remain "closely confined" in her bedroom for several weeks after giving birth. But Lucretia believed that childbearing was a natural act, one that should not be regarded as a sickness. So the day after Anna was born, Lucretia was up and walking around the house, and later that week she felt well enough to go shopping. At the marketplace she endured the stares and whispers of more frivolous "society" women who felt it was improper for a woman to appear physically strong. Lucretia just laughed: "[I am] classified among the Indians for so rash an act!" she told a friend.

The manufacturing business remained slow, and James grew increasingly worried. Despite Lucretia's thriftiness, they were still unable to accumulate any savings. Their circumstances were further complicated by Lucretia's becoming pregnant again when little Anna was only sixteen months old. Convinced that their financial situation would not improve in Philadelphia, James accepted a job at a cotton mill owned by his uncle, Richard Mott, in Mamaroneck, New York. Reluctantly, Lucretia packed their few belongings, said goodbye to her family, accompanied James to New York, and moved in with her in-laws.

CHAPTER 5

Lucretia's Gift

O n July 23, 1814, Lucretia gave birth to a son, whom she named Thomas. The event seemed to lift James's sagging spirits and kindled a general "family rejoicing" in the Mott household. Lucretia wrote to her parents, saying that she felt "rather proud" to be the mother of such a "fat and healthy" boy. She recovered quickly and settled into a routine of child care and housekeeping.

Meanwhile, the war with the British continued, and American businesses remained depressed. The Motts, like most Quakers, were confirmed pacifists who believed that war was wrong under any circumstances. To protest the fighting, Lucretia helped Uncle Richard Mott assemble "peace almanacs" (calendars decorated with anti-war sentiments), which "he gave away to neighbors and friends." Years later, Lucretia would take a more active role in promoting nonviolence.

The war with the British was adding to James Mott's

struggle to support his young family. The war had reduced trade with European markets, and his Uncle Richard's cotton business was failing; finally, his uncle had to let him go. Fortunately, James had heard about a job in a wholesale store back in Philadelphia, so he and Lucretia packed up and returned to her family's city — and her family's house. Lucretia was back in time to help prepare for and attend her sister Eliza's wedding in November. Eliza's new husband was a young gentleman named Benjamin Yarnell, "son of one of the most respected Quaker families in Philadelphia."

The happiness surrounding the couple was contagious, yet Lucretia's father appeared deeply troubled. Anna Coffin explained why: The nail business had gone bankrupt, and Thomas had loaned a large sum of money to a friend who had been unable to pay it back. Now the Coffins were deeply in debt. "The story is all over town," Anna told Lucretia sadly.

Lucretia loved and respected her father, yet she was angry with him, too. It seems that he had deliberately disregarded her mother's wise advice to keep his money and to sell out of the nail business. "It wasn't fair," Lucretia thought, "that women should suffer the consequences of decisions in which they had no voice." Many years later, when Lucretia became a leader in the struggle for women's rights, she made women's economic independence a top priority.

Thomas Coffin took his failure to heart. His health suffered, and he became seriously ill with typhus. He died early in 1815, his debts still unpaid. Though Lucretia was distraught over her father's death, her main concern was for her mother: How would Anna get the money she needed to send Lucretia's younger brother and sisters to Quaker schools? How would she support herself and her family and pay off the debt that Thomas had left her?

But Lucretia needn't have worried. That spring, Anna Coffin opened a shop in Philadelphia similar to the one she had owned on Nantucket. Women shopkeepers were "a rarity" in Philadelphia, but Anna's capacity for hard work and her innate business sense made her venture a success. She gradually paid off the family debt and had enough left over to send Thomas, Mary, and Martha to Quaker boarding schools.

Lucretia's husband, who was again out of work, also decided to try his hand at retailing, but his store fared poorly. Eventually he "was obliged to sell out at a considerable loss." Deeply discouraged, he accepted a job as a clerk on Wall Street in New York City. The job was secure, but less profitable than he had hoped.

Meanwhile, Lucretia began thinking about following her mother's example. Why shouldn't she contribute to the household income? Being a full-time housewife made her a bit restless, and besides, there was a job available for her: working with Rebecca Bunker, a niece of her mother's, "who had been hired to open a school in connection with the Pine Street Meeting." Lucretia also found a local merchant who was willing to hire

James at the same rate he was being paid in New York. So Lucretia wrote to James, explaining why she thought he should take the job back home. He happily agreed, and soon after he returned to Philadelphia, Lucretia went to work.

In March of 1817, Rebecca Bunker opened a "Select School for Girls" with Lucretia as her assistant. Lucretia approached this new venture with her usual abundant energy. Each morning she left Anna and Thomas in the care of her mother or sister and set off for work. Accompanied by Rebecca, she covered the several miles between her home and the school at a brisk pace. "Our walk is long," she told Ann Mott. "And, as there are two sessions, we take our dinner with us; but if we can get a large school, we shall not mind the long walk."

The school offered courses in reading, writing, arithmetic, and French. Lessons were conducted in small groups, and a "gentle firmness" was employed in matters of discipline. Unlike other early nineteenth-century schools, where switches were commonly used and spankings were frequent, this school strictly prohibited physical punishment of any sort.

Lucretia enjoyed her new endeavor, but this happy time was soon marred by tragedy. In the spring of 1817, she faced one of the greatest spiritual challenges of her lifetime. Both she and her little Thomas came down with high fevers. They battled the illness together, but only Lucretia recovered. Thomas grew steadily worse, and James and Lucretia "hovered over his bedside as he fought for breath." But it was no use. Within the week, Lucretia's "beautiful, rosy, healthy Tommy" was dead.

Although it was a glorious spring in Philadelphia, Lucretia's days seemed long and dark. She sometimes felt overwhelmed by Tommy's death, and she remained "so pale and quiet" that James feared that she might never fully recover. She performed her household duties in her usual efficient manner, but it appeared that she had lost her zest for life. Her mother and her sister Eliza comforted her as best they could, offering their sympathy, helping with the housework, and caring for little Anna.

As the weeks went by, Lucretia wrestled with her sorrow. But she returned to her position at the school, which no doubt helped her cope with her grief. The school was soon regarded as "one of the better institutions of its type in Philadelphia." Lucretia was proud of this success, and felt useful in her role as a classroom teacher. She had read a great deal when she had been home with her children, and now teaching gave her an outlet for her restless intellect. Whenever she had a few moments to herself, she sat down at her desk with a new book. As a student at Nine Partners she had done some "very serious reading"; now she began to study the Bible systematically.

As the months wore on, Lucretia continued to struggle with her loss. The knowledge that others had endured a similar tragedy (the death of children was common in the nineteenth century) did little to dispel her grief. But her rigorous study of the Bible was a help to her. Increasingly, she turned to the Scriptures to try to understand why God had taken Tommy. She prayed earnestly for the strength to endure her suffering and for the understanding that would lead to an acceptance of God's will.

This period of intense suffering and vulnerability served to increase Lucretia's faith. "Under the solemn influence of this bereavement she was led into a deeper religious feeling," wrote one of her grandchildren. "When [I] asked her, in [her] old age, how it happened that she became a preacher in the Society, she said, with tears, even then, that her grief at the dear boy's death turned her mind that way."

In the spring of 1818, at a Meeting of the Women Friends of the Western District of Philadelphia, Lucretia made her first public address. After sitting silently on the wooden bench of the Meetinghouse, awaiting divine inspiration, she rose slowly and spoke:

As all our efforts to resist temptation and overcome the world prove fruitless, unless aided by Thy Holy Spirit, enable us to approach Thy Throne, and ask of Thee the blessing of Thy preservation from all evil, that we may be wholly devoted to Thee and Thy glorious cause.

These words testified to Lucretia's belief that "a complete and unquestioning faith in God's omnipotence" was necessary in order to endure the trials of life. Her statement was brief, but she delivered it with such poise and eloquence that the elders encouraged her to express her thoughts more frequently. Buoyed by their encouragement, Lucretia became more vocal during Meeting, and she spoke with authority whenever the Spirit moved her. Word began to travel through the city that Mrs. Mott had a particular gift for receiving divine inspiration and for articulating these revelations to others.

Accordingly, in January of 1821, Lucretia was formally recognized as a minister. Although female ministers were common in the Society of Friends, it was rare that someone so young (Lucretia was only 28 years old at the time of her designation) should be so honored. Quaker ministers were expected to lead their congregations in discussion, to serve as role models for other members, and, if so inclined, to travel and preach at other Meetings.

In the nineteenth century, an equal number of men and women became traveling ministers, or "Public Friends." They belonged to an elite group of individuals who, though scattered across the United States, were to have an enormous impact on the social reforms in the developing nation. According to Margaret Hope Bacon, "Forty-eight percent of the women who made a name for themselves in American history in the ministry were of Quaker background." Because Quakers believed that men and women should have "an equal standing . . . in determining the affairs of the church," becoming a minister became "a vehicle for self-expression which enabled [Quaker women] to play a role in the life of their community."

During the early 1820s, Lucretia nurtured her growing family (daughter Maria had been born in 1818; a son, the second Thomas, was born in 1823) and gained confidence in her preaching. She continued to read voraciously, a habit that fed her intellect and introduced her to subjects which she later addressed in her sermons. She learned about Quaker history through the writings of the English preacher George Fox, who had founded the Society of Friends in the mid-seventeenth century. Her thoughts on the issues of freedom and equality were inspired by the writings of Quaker colonialist William Penn.

It was the sermons by Congregationalist minister William Channing, however, that compelled Lucretia to re-examine her religious views. Channing, like Penn, was a lover of liberty and a staunch opponent of both slavery and war. The sermon he had preached in Baltimore in May of 1819 had sparked a heated controversy among American Christians. Channing believed in the inherent dignity of the human soul and opposed the Puritan idea that people were inherently wicked. He thought that contemporary Christians should use reason (a God-given gift) to modify religious traditions that were harmful or outmoded. He claimed that when people ignored reason and blindly followed powerful religious leaders, social conflict and oppression were bound to result.

Channing's philosophy appealed to Lucretia, whose own ability to apply reason to divine inspiration had won her a prominent position within the Quaker community. Like Channing, she believed that the solutions to life's challenges lay within people themselves. "Mighty powers are at work in the world, and who shall stay them?" Channing had asked. When Lucretia preached, she warned others against relying too heavily on traditional thinking when faced with modern social problems: "Let us not hesitate to aspire to be the messiahs of our age," she urged.

Inspired by Channing and other contemporary thinkers, Lucretia incorporated their ideas into her sermons and speeches. She quickly developed a reputation for tackling controversial issues in a rational, straightforward, yet uncompromising manner. When the elders of the Twelfth Street Meeting (where the Motts were members) threatened to disown a member for allowing her daughter to marry a non-Quaker, Lucretia rose immediately to her defense. Such an action, she felt, was "a denial of the very tenets which Quakerism embraced." When other members were actually disowned because they had attended a lecture on controversial educational reforms, Lucretia called it "outrageous." Believing that "truth would [always] prevail over error," she thought it ridiculous to "punish people simply for their willingness to listen to new ideas." Were the elders now ready to condemn the same kind of free thinking that had first inspired the formation of the Society of Friends? she asked. Had they forgotten that the earliest Quakers had followed a similar process when they sought to break away from the suffocating restrictions of Puritanism?

Although irritated by Lucretia's liberal views, the elders had difficulty refuting her arguments. She was so widely read, so articulate, and possessed such a thorough understanding of both traditional and contemporary philosophy that her position in such controversies always seemed, in the end, the reasonable one. Yet despite her belief in reason, she depended on "a constant relationship between herself and the Divine Spirit. . . . She worshipped always . . . seeking the Divine Will and practicing Holy Obedience."

It was during this time that Lucretia also read *Vindication of the Rights of Women* by the English author Mary Wollstonecraft (1759-97). Written in 1792, this well-constructed, highly controversial work had a profound effect on Lucretia's thinking, and, much later, on her work on behalf of women's rights. Lucretia's copy of the book became one of her most cherished possessions. Family legend maintains that she kept it on a table in the front parlor of her home for more than forty years, lending it only to her closest friends.

In *Vindication,* Wollstonecraft argued for the liberation of female minds through equal educational and professional opportunities:

I [am] . . . against the custom of confining girls to their [sewing], and shutting them out from all political and civil employments; for by thus narrowing their minds they are rendered unfit to fulfill the peculiar duties which nature has assigned them. . . . Make [women] free, and they will quickly become wise and virtuous, as men become more so; for the improvement must be mutual, or the injustice [to] which one half of the human race [is] obliged to submit . . . will [continue].

Lucretia had been raised to believe that men's and women's minds were equal. Unfortunately, most people in the nineteenth century did not share this conviction. In *Vindication,* Wollstonecraft challenged the commonly held belief that a woman's intellectual capacity was, by nature, much smaller than a man's. Moreover, she challenged that belief "at a time when suggesting women could reason was revolutionary." Because Lucretia herself was blessed with the gift of reason and knew that other women were too, the book touched a chord deep in her soul. Here again, she thought, was another "wrong crying to be righted."

❂   ❂   ❂

By 1824, James was doing reasonably well in the wholesale business. His salary was now more than a thousand dollars a year, and this, combined with Lucretia's frugal habits, afforded them financial security. At long last, James and Lucretia were able to set up housekeeping on their own; they moved to a house on Sansom Street. (Anna Coffin had given up her shop and now ran a boardinghouse.) In 1825 James and Lucretia had another child, Elizabeth, making Lucretia the proud mother of four. She seemed to have recovered from the loss of her first son, but family members noticed that she "could [not] speak of him without tears coming to her eyes."

But during this time of growth and relative prosperity, tragedy struck again. First, Lucretia's older sister Sarah died after a bad fall. Because Sarah was handicapped, details of her death, as of the rest of her life, remain sketchy. Then Lucretia's younger sister Mary died in childbirth, and the baby boy, who was sickly, died shortly thereafter, leaving his older sister, Anna, an orphan. Lucretia wasted no time in adopting the little girl into her own family, for she believed that "one person's troubles were shouldered by all." Soon afterward, Martha's husband, Peter Pelham, died of a fever, leaving Lucretia's youngest sister a widow at nineteen and the single mother of their daughter, Marianne. Lucretia also welcomed them into the big house on Sansom Street, where Marianne was unofficially adopted into the Mott family.

The family mourned these multiple losses, which served to draw the surviving members even closer together. In the wake of these personal tragedies, Lucretia focused on her spiritual life and her "continuing search for the path of duty." She became increasingly concerned with larger social issues, especially that of slavery. Several years earlier, she had accompanied another Quaker woman to Virginia, where she had witnessed the horrible conditions under which enslaved black families lived and worked. She saw hungry children, poorly clothed, picking cotton for hours in the blistering sun. She heard stories of men and women being beaten by their owners for minor transgressions, and of parents being separated from their children on the auction block. "The [plight] of these poor slaves was indeed affecting," Lucretia wrote, "though we were told their situation [elsewhere] was rendered less deplorable, by kind treatment from their masters." Despite evidence that this was true, Lucretia remained appalled by the fact that one human being could "own" another and thereby completely determine his or her fate.

And the slavery problem was evident in Philadelphia, even though Pennsylvania was a free state (a state that outlawed slavery). As biographer Margaret Hope Bacon explains, "There were often disturbances on the city streets as slaves visiting the city with their Southern masters tried to escape. . . . Sometimes, too, a crowd would gather as a slave kidnaper tried to hustle a free black out of the city, intending to take him South and pass him off as an escaped slave." The blacks in Philadelphia were free, but few of them lived well. Although a few black families managed successful businesses and earned a decent living, most were plagued by poverty and prejudice.

In response to the injustice of slavery, abolitionist societies were springing up in many of the major northern cities. The Pennsylvania Abolition Society (a more conservative group than the Pennsylvania Anti-Slavery Society) had been created in Philadelphia in 1775, and James Mott was an active member. (James later served as president and helped to establish a school for the children of free blacks.)

Lucretia shared her husband's concern for the welfare of free blacks. Many were in desperate need of financial assistance, nutritional guidance, education, and job training. It was her desire to try to address these problems that first propelled Lucretia into the arena of social reform. She and other concerned women formed "one of the first women's political groups" in America, the Philadelphia Female Anti-Slavery Society. Nearly all of the original members were Quakers, but there was "a sprinkling of Presbyterians and Unitarians." Black women as well as white participated in the meetings, signed petitions, and organized fund-raising activities. Lucretia was elected corresponding clerk, and she co-authored their constitution: "We deem it our duty as professing Christians," she wrote, "to manifest our abhorrence of the flagrant injustice and deep sin of slavery by united and vigorous [actions]." The women agreed that steps must be taken toward total abolition, but they emphasized "the improvement of the social, economic, and educational standards of the free Negro population of Philadelphia."

As her involvement in this organization grew and her friendships with black women deepened, Lucretia became even more aware of the insidious prejudices that prevented blacks from gaining equal rights in politics, education, and employment. They were not permitted to vote, serve on juries, send their children to public schools, or live in white neighborhoods.

Determined to "break down the segregated social patterns" that existed within the community, she frequently invited her black friends to dinner and accompanied them to social functions in the city. She preached at several black churches in Philadelphia, where her "philosophical" yet "devout" sermons inspired congregations.

Lucretia's decision to eliminate the use of slave-made products in her home was further evidence of her commitment. The inspiration for this action had come from a traveling journalist and concerned abolitionist named Benjamin Lundy, who visited Philadelphia in the mid-1820s. During his stay in the city, he lectured publicly on the evils of slavery and argued for a boycott of products that were the direct result of slave labor. Lundy's words roused Lucretia's conscience, and she resolved immediately to "make things honest" in her household. Products such as sugar, molasses, cotton, and even writing paper (made partially of cotton fibers) would have to be sacrificed for the cause. "It was like parting with the right hand or the right eye," she wrote, ". . . but I yielded to obligation. For nearly forty years, whatever I did was under the conviction that it was wrong to partake of [these]."

Lucretia's children occasionally rebelled against her decision. "Free products" were not only harder to get but also less desirable. Her daughters "mumbled about their [cotton] free muslins and ginghams [which] could seldom be called handsome." They described candies made without sugar as "an abomination," and they complained that their birthday parties no longer featured ice cream, a delicacy for which Philadelphia was becoming famous.

Lucretia's commitment forced James to consider how his mercantile business might be indirectly supporting slavery. More than half of his profits came from the sale of cotton produced in the South through slave labor. Abolitionists urged a boycott on all cotton products, but James did not participate at first for fear of bankruptcy. But at Lucretia's urging and after much soul-searching, he eventually decided to stop selling cotton. Following Scripture's advice that one should "be careful to do what is right in the eyes of everybody" (Romans 12:17), he switched to selling wool. The change cleared James's conscience and, happily, proved to have no ill effect on the family's income.

Lucretia's commitment to abolition affected every aspect of her life, including her Quaker ministry. When she rose to speak in Meeting, she asked members to examine their hearts and to lend their support to the anti-slavery movement. This frequently angered the elders, who thought that she was "mingling too much with the world's people" and "ought to stick to more

69

spiritual subjects." But Lucretia continued to speak out, reminding them of the Quakers' long history in the anti-slavery movement.

American Quakers had begun their public opposition to slavery in the late seventeenth century. In 1688, the Germantown (Pennsylvania) Friends made the following protest:

> There is a liberty of conscience here which is right and reasonable, and there ought to be likewise a liberty of the body, except for evil doers, which is another case. But to bring men [here], or to rob and sell them against their will, we stand against.

Throughout the 1700s, the Society of Friends brought increasing pressure upon its members who had ties to slavery (those who owned slaves or who otherwise participated in the slave trade) to mend their ways. The Society's plea was not entirely successful, however, for only those whose businesses would not suffer gave up their slaves. Many refused to do so because their livelihood was so thoroughly tied to the institution of slavery that they risked putting themselves into debt. As a result, the official policy remained limited to "advising Friends not to encourage the importation of more slaves."

Toward the end of the eighteenth century, anti-slavery sentiment grew stronger. In 1775, the first recorded abolitionist meeting, organized and run by the Quakers, took place in Philadelphia. Five years later,

Pennsylvania outlawed slavery and began to establish schools for children of free blacks. In 1808, when Lucretia was only fifteen years old, the United States had outlawed the importation of slaves.

Total abolition seemed the next logical — and morally necessary — step. But as Lucretia would soon discover, the road to freedom for blacks would be a long and difficult one.

CHAPTER 6

Bitter Conflicts

A growing "spirit of division" characterized the Quaker church in the 1820s. Friends divided themselves into two groups, each having a different opinion about the future of the Society. At the heart of the controversy was the ministry of Elias Hicks, the country farmer who had preached at Nine Partners during Lucretia's school years. According to Hicks, modern Quakers were slowly moving away from the simple philosophy and straightforward style of worship that had been the hallmark of their founding members. Meetings had become too rigid, he said, and the elders wielded too much power.

Hicks advocated "a rebirth of the spirit of Christ" in the Quaker church and a return to the more democratic philosophy of the early Friends. His views appealed to many of the younger, more liberal Quakers, and by the mid-1820s he had gained hundreds of followers. These "Hicksites" were in favor of reducing the amount of religious dogma in their worship; they believed that each individual should rely on his or her "Divine Inner Light" as a guide to moral behavior.

The "Orthodox" group, which included most members of the Motts' Twelfth Street Meeting in Philadelphia, wanted to maintain the elders' authority and were less inclined to modify religious traditions (they denied members the right to marry non-Quakers or to form friendships with those whose ideas were considered socially "radical"). In their opinion, Hicks "stressed the Light Within too much and the importance of the Bible and the life of the historic Jesus too little." Orthodox members had the full support of the English Friends, who labeled Hicks a heretic and refused to recognize his followers as church members. Names of known Hicksites that appeared on U.S. documents sent to England were marked with asterisks and each one dismissed with the phrase "erroneously described as a member of the Society of Friends."

The Quaker church was just one of many groups being torn apart by sweeping social changes occurring around this time. As economic and political climates shifted throughout the world, the power of traditional authorities decreased while the value of each individual gradually increased. In Europe, military monarchs were being overthrown and replaced by more democratic political systems. In America, newly formed states produced local governments that tried to accommodate the interests and needs — rural, urban, frontier — of their diverse citizenship.

The world's population continued to grow at a faster rate than ever before. Increasingly, families chose to forsake their small farms and move to the city in search of a less demanding livelihood. European immigrants arrived in America by the tens of thousands, fleeing wars, famine, and religious intolerance. This led inevitably to a sharing of ideas and a mixing of people from various cultures and ethnic backgrounds. Old ways of behaving yielded more easily to new ones as individuals struggled to form new communities and to build a better future for themselves and their children.

All of these developments strengthened the Hicksites' argument for increased tolerance and a wider distribution of authority within the Quaker church. Despite efforts to discourage change, Orthodox elders could not prevent the influx of new ideas that provoked more progressive members to question their authority.

In the midst of this quarreling, Lucretia found herself in a most peculiar position. As a designated minister, she was considered part of the lofty group of elders against whose authority the Hicksites were so loudly protesting. As an individual, however, Lucretia "deplored the petty bickering" and "was not in sympathy with [the elders'] attacks on Elias, nor the stern way in which they disowned so many good people." His daughters had been her schoolmates at Nine Partners, and Hicks himself had served as her role model for impassioned public speaking.

As the dispute over Hicks's teachings continued, Lucretia remained hopeful that his ideas might somehow be incorporated into the doctrine of the Society without causing a split in the church. By the mid-1820s, however, such a split seemed inevitable. The Motts found themselves facing the unenviable task of having to choose a side, a decision that would necessarily alienate them from relatives and acquaintances on the opposite one.

For James, the choice was clear. He had allied himself with Hicks from the very beginning, and so he had little trouble leaving the Orthodox Twelfth Street Meeting. In doing so, he incurred the wrath of his mother, Anne Mott, who for months thereafter "did not pay her usual visits (from New York), nor did she answer [his] letters." Despite her disapproval, however, James remained a devoted Hicksite. In a letter to his parents, he explained why: "I [believe] . . . that Elias is sound in the essential doctrines of Quakerism and Christianity; and the great opposition to him arises, in some, from a difference in sentiment on minor and unimportant subjects; and in others, from tradition in themselves."

Lucretia, on the other hand, needed more time to decide. Although she supported Hicks's ministry, she could not conceive of abandoning her beloved Twelfth Street Meeting. She had formed many close friendships there, and her preaching skills were highly regarded by the members.

Her internal struggle was complicated by external pressures from Friends on both sides. Already she was known as "the city's outstanding reform leader" (James was often called "Mr. Lucretia Mott"). Her spiritual insight and verbal eloquence were coveted by both Hicksite and Orthodox members, and both parties lobbied hard to win her allegiance. Lucretia despaired over this "party spirit," and later referred to this as "a time of [great] suffering." She craved peace and harmony above all, yet she felt as though she were trapped in a childish tug-of-war.

When Hicks preached in Philadelphia, the Motts welcomed him into their home. His visit confirmed their high opinion of him and drew Lucretia closer to a decision. "We have been much in his company, and find him the same consistent, exemplary man that he was many years ago," Lucretia wrote to Anne Mott. "I believe the criterion still remains, that 'the tree is known by its fruit.'"

At the Yearly Meeting of 1827, tensions within the Society came to a bitter climax. Because the Friends were unable to agree on a clerk to preside over the gathering, the separation became official. The Philadelphia Hicksites left the Orthodox group and held a separate Meeting in "temporary quarters" nearby. Here they made plans to build a large meetinghouse on Cherry Street that would hold their growing congregation.

This physical separation forced Lucretia's hand. After agonizing for months, she knew it was time to choose. "She prepared to join her husband," wrote her grand-daughter Anna Hallowell, "and make the social sacrifice [and endure] the disappointments, trials, and baptisms, that awaited her in the transfer of her right of member-ship." The Hicksites rejoiced when Lucretia first appeared at their temporary quarters. The most partisan Hicksites spread the message throughout the city: "Aha, we have Lucretia!"

Though outwardly relieved to have made her choice, Lucretia remained "troubled by the separation." Later, she recalled that "[it had felt] almost like death to be shut out of the [Twelfth Street] Meeting where I loved to go and [to] see the cold averted looks of Friends whose confidence I once enjoyed."

The event marked a turning point in Lucretia's life. During her first few years in the ministry, she had been "concerned with obedience to divine law and to the doctrines of her Society." Yet, as biographer Dorothy Sterling points out, "After watching [those] she respected battling over these doctrines, she no longer accepted them blindly." Unwittingly, the Orthodox elders had taught Lucretia an invaluable lesson regarding power and the use of authority. From this time on her motto became "Seek Truth for authority, not authority for Truth."

Lucretia now began working for the Hicksite branch of the Society of Friends. As biographer Margaret Hope Bacon explains, "She began on a small scale by visiting

all the families who were members of the new downtown Hicksite Monthly Meeting. . . . Lucretia went
from household to household to sit in the best parlor
with family members until she was moved to speak.
This first mission was a great success." Lucretia would
probably have gone on to undertake larger tasks, but
she discovered that she was pregnant "at the advanced
age of thirty-five."

In October of 1828, Lucretia's sixth and last child
was born. She named her Martha, after her youngest
sister, but family members nicknamed her Pattie.
("Grandmother Coffin" was probably not as close as
Lucretia would have liked. She had moved to Aurora,
New York, to help run a school there.) For the next two
years, Lucretia remained close to home and preached
only at local meetinghouses. Gradually she became accustomed to the new Cherry Street Meeting, and she
regrouped her energies for the challenges she knew lay
ahead. This pattern of temporary withdrawal into the
"safe" and simplified world of her family following a
period of upheaval or loss was one that Lucretia repeated frequently throughout her lifetime. "She drew
nourishment from her relationships," writes Margaret
Hope Bacon. "[Her] deep immersion in the lives of her
children and her closest friends gave her sanctuary, a
little Nantucket Island in a sea of troubles."

During Lucretia's self-imposed withdrawal from public
life, the anti-slavery movement continued to gain mo-

mentum. Always eager to do her share, Lucretia offered her house as a meeting place for leading abolitionists of the day. When Lucretia's sister Martha came from New York for a visit, she was shocked to find the house filled with strangers. "There are about fifty [here] counting our own family," she reported in a letter to her new husband David Wright. "For a while it was quite interesting. . . . The conversation then took a metaphysical turn on the subject of heaven and its opposite. . . . For the rest of the evening I amused myself with observing the company."

Over the course of the next decade, Lucretia frequently entertained abolitionists from Boston, Rhode Island, New York, and the surrounding counties of Pennsylvania. Men such as Benjamin Lundy (founder and editor of anti-slavery newspapers) and his colleague John Greenleaf Whittier (a New England poet and journal editor) received meals, lodging, and stimulating conversation whenever they visited the city. Philadelphia abolitionists such as James Forten (a successful black businessman), Charles Burleigh (a prominent writer and lecturer), and William Furness (a Unitarian minister and author) were also regular guests.

In addition to serving as a hub for visiting abolitionists, the Motts' home was a magnet for the destitute. Word spread throughout the city that the down-and-out "could always count on something to eat and perhaps a few coins at Lucretia's door." As a member of the Society for the Relief and Employment of the Poor,

Lucretia cooked meals for the elderly, distributed used household items and clothing to the poor, and helped the unemployed find work.

Hundreds of middle-class women were becoming involved in charitable societies such as this one, but public protest and political activism remained almost exclusively male activities. In these early years of social activism, there were many intelligent, ambitious, and energetic women who worked behind the scenes. Their role was restricted to giving emotional support (as well as the necessary lodging and meals) to their fathers, husbands, or brothers whose voices were heard in the city squares and whose articles were read in national journals. It would be another decade before female abolitionists such as Abby Kelley, Angelina and Sarah Grimké, Lydia Maria Child, and Maria Chapman would make their voices heard, exerting a public influence equal to that of the men.

In May of 1830, Lucretia was made clerk of the Philadelphia Women's Yearly Meeting. Just days later she received a copy of a letter written by John Comly, the clerk of the Philadelphia Men's Meeting. It was a response to the Orthodox English Friends, who claimed that American Hicksites — including the entire membership of Philadelphia's Cherry Street Meeting — lacked the convictions of true Christians and were seeking to destroy religious traditions. In his response, Comly claimed that the difference between the Hicksites and the Orthodox lay in the latter's "exercise of an oppressive authority within the church." He also declared that "the history of the birth, life, acts, death, and resurrection of the Holy Jesus, as in the volume of the book it is written of him, we reverently believe." This, Lucretia saw, was a clear repudiation of Hicks, who stressed the Divine Light that burned in every believer, and who insisted that "it was the inward Christ that mattered, not the outward events of his birth and death."

Lucretia was torn. This wasn't a letter she could support, yet she would have to read it as clerk of the Women's Meeting. And read it she did — but immediately thereafter she turned over the meeting to the recording clerk and spoke against the letter. Some of the women secretly agreed with her, but in the end the consensus was that the letter be signed. This was another duty that fell to Lucretia as clerk, but before returning the letter to Comly she made some corrections to it. Comly didn't like being edited, and he didn't like the fact that Lucretia had spoken against the letter. He was further annoyed when the London Yearly Meeting "returned the letter with the word *mendacity* written over it." The English Quakers "went so far as to place the major burden of guilt upon the shoulders of Lucretia Mott." Yet, as Otelia Cromwell points out in her biography, this seemed only to heighten Lucretia's acclaim among the Hicksites:

> From the number and significance of the offices [that she] held, one may see that . . . she was accorded no

limited measure of responsibility and regard. . . . For five years she was Clerk to the Women's Yearly Meeting, for two years she was treasurer, she was almost regularly a representative . . . from the Quarterly Meeting of Abington, and she continued to be placed on committees chosen to write . . . to Meetings in New York, Indiana, Ohio, and Baltimore.

In August of 1830, Lucretia and James Mott had a young "stranger" visit them: William Lloyd Garrison. He worked for an anti-slavery newspaper in Boston run by Benjamin Lundy, a friend of the Motts, and Lundy had encouraged Garrison to visit the couple on his way home. During dinner with James and Lucretia, Garrison outlined the message about abolition he felt compelled to deliver. Would the Motts help him do it?

Convinced by his argument, the Motts agreed. Lucretia arranged for him to speak at Philadelphia's Franklin Institute and got an audience together — mainly Quakers. Garrison advocated immediate emancipation and called the slaveowners "man-stealers," but he blunted the power of his speech by reading it from notes. Newspaper reporters later described the speech as "uninviting and defective."

The Motts were among those in the audience, and though they were impressed by Garrison's courage and commitment, they agreed with the paper's assessment of his delivery. The next day Lucretia invited Garrison over for tea and offered him some advice: "If thou expects to set forth thy cause by word of mouth," she told him, "thou must learn to lay aside thy papers and speak from the heart."

Garrison took her advice: from then on, he delivered his speeches with more passion and self-assurance. And January 1, 1831, saw the publication of the first issue of the *Liberator*, a weekly anti-slavery newspaper of which Garrison was the editor. "I do not want to think or speak or write with moderation [on the issue of slavery]. . . . I will not retreat a single inch — and I will be HEARD!" he wrote.

By the time Pattie was a few years old, Lucretia was also becoming anxious to be heard, to travel in the ministry. With the full support of the Cherry Street Meeting, she left her mother in charge of her children and household (Anna Coffin had returned to Philadelphia to live with the Motts) and set off for New York. Much "to the horror" of her Philadelphia acquaintances, she ignored the custom of taking a chaperone and insisted on making the first leg of the trip alone. She stayed in Aurora, where she visited her sister Martha and preached at several Meetings nearby. Following this trip, she made an extended journey through the Delaware Valley area to visit Friends in their homes and to preach at Meetings in New Jersey, Delaware, and southeastern Pennsylvania.

James joined her whenever possible, though his thriving mercantile business prevented him from leaving Philadelphia for more than a few weeks at a time.

When together, the couple traveled "from town to town in an open buggy" and stayed in the homes of fellow Quakers. Lucretia's reputation as an eloquent spokesperson preceded her, and meetinghouses were filled to capacity wherever she went. In her sermons, she urged people to become "vessels of the Holy Spirit in works of reform" and warned them that "the living spirit of religion must not be confused with the forms that had once cloaked it."

Lucretia had no sympathy for those who were apathetic toward the very real problems — poverty, conflict, prejudice, slavery — that plagued society. In her traveling ministry, she committed herself to rousing Friends into social action. "To be like Jesus," she said, "was to meet human need, both physical and spiritual . . . [for] he himself never separated his inner self from his outward duties."

CHAPTER 7

New Voices

In 1833, Great Britain abolished slavery in the West Indies (a group of islands southeast of the United States in the Caribbean Sea). The British government compensated slaveholders for their loss, and granted free slaves the option of becoming paid apprentices.

The action prompted U.S. abolitionists to increase their anti-slavery efforts. John Greenleaf Whittier, editor of the anti-slavery journal called *Pennsylvania Freeman*, wrote and published "Justice and Expediency," a provocative pamphlet that put forth "a powerful argument for anti-slavery." His colleague, William Lloyd Garrison, continued to publish strident editorials in the *Liberator*, his widely read anti-slavery newspaper. Through his tireless work on behalf of the New England Anti-Slavery Society (which he had founded in Boston in 1832), Garrison had won thousands of converts to the cause of abolition.

Still, he felt he could do more. Inspired by Britain's

declaration, Garrison organized a national convention to be held in December of 1833. He asked that each of the northern states elect delegates and send them to Philadelphia, where they would form a national organization.

Upon learning that James had been one of the men selected to represent Pennsylvania, Lucretia prepared to host delegates who would be arriving from out-of-town. The Motts' hospitality had become legendary; as one relative observed, "It was not unusual for thirty people to sit down to dinner [in their home]."

With the help of her mother and daughters, Lucretia oversaw the necessary preparations. The women scrubbed floors, laid down new rugs (which Lucretia, who was always thrifty, had made from scraps of material), washed sheets, made beds, and hung fresh curtains. When the guests arrived, they were shown to their rooms, offered tea and cakes, and handed pamphlets on anti-slavery. Lucretia also invited Garrison, who was staying at a hotel, to come for tea the next day, and to bring any friends along. After she issued a few more invitations, she realized she would have fifty guests.

On December 4, the opening day of the convention, Lucretia "spent the morning . . . shopping and baking." After a short trip to the Cherry Street market, she returned home laden with bags and boxes. Her good-natured laugh announced her arrival as she struggled onto the front porch, clutching cartons of pickled herring, spiced calves' tongue, oysters, and cheese. After unloading her purchases in the spacious kitchen, she set about preparing a hearty meal. The smell of the bubbling stews and baking bread recalled memories of her Nantucket childhood, when the women would prepare a feast to celebrate the sailors' return. "The Nantucket women understood to perfection the art of cookery," wrote Lucretia's granddaughter: "how to make much out of very little, as well as to make the most of much . . . [and] rejoiced in occasions which called forth their culinary skill."

Like her Nantucket ancestors, Lucretia relished the creativity involved in preparing delicious food as well as the challenge of cooking for a large group. Over the years, she gained a reputation as an excellent cook and an efficient and gracious hostess. "Mrs. Mott is a great abolitionist, but she's a fine cook, too," said abolitionist Daniel Neall when he introduced her at an anti-slavery meeting. And in a letter from Philadelphia to his paper, Garrison wrote, "I was indebted to . . . Lucretia Mott for a homelike reception, affectionate and delightful. . . . My regard for [her] amounts to unfeigned veneration."

As she tended to her household, Lucretia was fully aware that her role, though appreciated and necessary, was secondary to those of the male delegates. Although equally well-educated and perhaps even more well-read than some of the delegates, she seemed content to play the part of nurturer to the speech-and-policy makers. (The first women's rights convention, which Lucretia would be instrumental in organizing, was still fifteen years away.)

Yet, in the midst of the dizzying rounds of household chores that were necessary to keep her guests well fed and comfortable, Lucretia managed to make a subtle statement on behalf of her gender. On the table in the front parlor next to the piles of pamphlets lay a metal seal that was used to mark anti-slavery documents. The official version, used by the abolitionists, pictured a black man in chains, kneeling, hands clasped together in prayer, under the words "Am I not a Man and a Brother?" On Lucretia's seal, however, a woman was pictured underneath the inscription "Am I not a Woman and a Sister?" When her nephew Thomas teased her about wanting to make "an impression," Lucretia smiled a conspiratorial smile and went about her chores.

But Lucretia was to become more important to the convention than she could have guessed. The day after she had given the tea, the visiting abolitionists, out of gratitude for her hospitality, invited Lucretia and the other ladies of the house to observe the convention proceedings. Lucretia accepted eagerly, as did her mother and her oldest daughter Anna (now married to Edward Hopper of Philadelphia). Lucretia and "the two Annas" quickly tied on their gray bonnets and dashed to the convention hall on Fifth Street. "I wanted to go here and there, and notify [other] persons to [come]," Lucretia recalled later, "but I was asked not to use up the whole morning."

This portrait of Lucretia by William Henry Furness Jr.
captures both her beauty and her spiritual strength.
Courtesy of the Friends Historical Library of Swarthmore College

Two very powerful — and enduring — influences on Lucretia's life:
her mother, Anna Coffin, and the island of Nantucket.
Portrait of Anna Coffin courtesy of the Friends Historical Library of Swarthmore
College; southeastern view of Nantucket drawn by J.W. Barber, engraved by S.E.
Brown, Boston; courtesy of the Nantucket Historical Association

NINE PARTNERS BOARDING SCHOOL. (FROM A SKETCH BY ALEX. H COFFIN, 1820.)

The Meetinghouse at Nine Partners (*above*) and the Boarding
School (*below*). Here the young Lucretia received an excellent
education — and also met her future husband, James Mott.
Lithograph from a sketch by A.H. Coffin, 1820; courtesy
of the Friends Historical Library of Swarthmore College

Elias Hicks, whose impassioned speeches at Nine Partners concerning the injustice of slavery awakened Lucretia's social conscience.
Engraving of Elias Hicks, published by Edward Hopper, drawn by H. Liman, engraved by Peter Maverick; courtesy of the Friends Historical Library of Swarthmore College

When Lucretia was a young woman, she was strongly influenced by the sermons of Congregationalist minister William Channing, who vigorously opposed both slavery and war.
Painting by S. Gambardella (1839), photographed by H.G. Smith, Boston; courtesy of the Sophia Smith Collection, Smith College

(*Above*) When Lucretia began to "expound" at Meeting, she incorporated the ideas of Channing and others into her sermons and speeches. She frequently spoke against slavery.
Piece entitled "Moved by the Spirit" by C. Turner, 1907; courtesy of the Friends Historical Library of Swarthmore College

(*Below*) Cherry Street Meetinghouse. James and Lucretia joined this meeting when the controversy over Elias Hicks's teachings caused a rift among liberal and conservative Quakers.
Courtesy of the Friends Historical Library of Swarthmore College

Two very vocal opponents of slavery: William Lloyd Garrison *(right)* and Frederick Douglass *(below)*. When Lucretia spoke against slavery in Ohio in 1847, both Garrison and Douglass, a former slave, were in the audience. Afterward Douglass wrote, "Her truthful words came down upon the audience like drops of summer rain." Picture of Garrison by M.C. Torrey, courtesy of the Friends Historical Library of Swarthmore College; picture of Douglass courtesy of UPI/Bettman

Sojourner Truth, a freed slave who was a prominent activist in both the abolitionist and women's rights movements. When she spoke in Philadelphia, she was a guest of the Motts.
Courtesy of the Bentley Historical Library, University of Michigan

The seal that Lucretia used to stamp anti-slavery documents. With this stamp she made a strong statement both about abolition and about women's rights.
Courtesy of the Historical Society of Pennsylvania

The burning of Pennsylvania Hall, the site of the Second
Anti-Slavery Convention of American Women in May of 1838.
This violent act pained Lucretia deeply.
Courtesy of the Quaker Collection, Haverford College

The Executive Committee of the Pennsylvania Anti-Slavery Society.
(Lucretia and James sit in the front row to the far right.)
For Lucretia, the rights of slaves and the rights of women
became increasingly intertwined.
Courtesy of the Quaker Collection, Haverford College

Mary Wollstonecraft, whose *Vindication of the Rights of Women* greatly influenced Lucretia as a young woman.
Photo of etching by A. L. Merritt, courtesy of the Sophia Smith Collection, Smith College

Elizabeth Cady Stanton. She and Lucretia became friends — and resolved to become advocates of women's rights — when they met in 1840 at the first World's Anti-Slavery Convention in London.
Courtesy of the Schlesinger Library, Radcliffe College

THE FIRST CONVENTION

EVER CALLED TO DISCUSS THE

Civil and Political Rights of Women,

SENECA FALLS, N. Y., JULY 19, 20, 1848.

WOMAN'S RIGHTS CONVENTION.

A Convention to discuss the social, civil, and religious condition and rights of woman will be held in the Wesleyan Chapel, at Seneca Falls, N. Y., on Wednesday and Thursday, the 19th and 20th of July current; commencing at 10 o'clock A. M. During the first day the meeting will be exclusively for women, who are earnestly invited to attend. The public generally are invited to be present on the second day, when Lucretia Mott, of Philadelphia, and other ladies and gentlemen, will address the Convention.[*]

[*] This call was published in the *Seneca County Courier*, July 14, 1848, without any signatures. The movers of this Convention, who drafted the call, the declaration and resolutions were Elizabeth Cady Stanton, Lucretia Mott, Martha C. Wright, Mary Ann McClintock, and Jane C. Hunt.

A watershed event: the announcement of the first women's rights convention, featuring Lucretia as one of the speakers.
Courtesy of the Sophia Smith Collection, Smith College

Sarah (*right*) and
Angelina Grimké
(*below*), both of
whom wrote and
spoke passionately
about women's rights.
Pictures courtesy of the
Bettman Archive

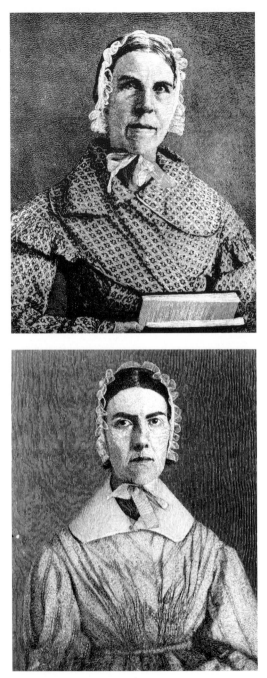

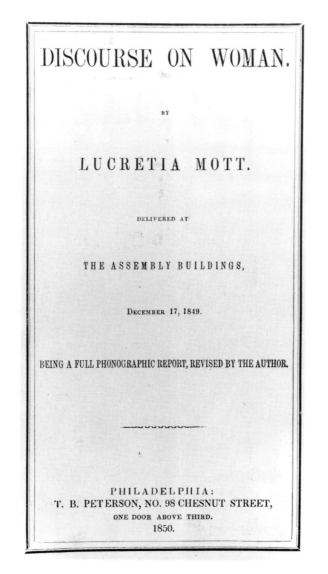

DISCOURSE ON WOMAN.

BY

LUCRETIA MOTT.

DELIVERED AT

THE ASSEMBLY BUILDINGS,

DECEMBER 17, 1849.

BEING A FULL PHONOGRAPHIC REPORT, REVISED BY THE AUTHOR.

PHILADELPHIA:
T. B. PETERSON, NO. 98 CHESNUT STREET,
ONE DOOR ABOVE THIRD.
1850.

Like the Grimké sisters, Lucretia became increasingly well known for her passionate defense of women's rights. Her "Discourse on Woman," an address she gave on "the true and proper position of women," was subsequently printed as a pamphlet that circulated for years.
Courtesy of the Sophia Smith Collection, Smith College

(Right) A portrait of James and Lucretia taken about 1842. Their 56-year marriage was marked by love, devotion, and mutual support.
Daguerreotype by Lagenheim, ca. 1842; courtesy of the Friends Historical Library of Swarthmore College

(Below) "Roadside," the farmhouse that the Motts moved to in 1856. Although Lucretia and James lived outside the city, they didn't retire from their causes.
Photograph by John W. Hurn, courtesy of the Friends Historical Library of Swarthmore College

(Left) George Fox, who founded the Society of Friends in the midseventeenth century. (No likenesses of Fox were produced during his lifetime. This lithograph is by A. Newsam, supplied courtesy of the Friends Historical Library of Swarthmore College.)

(Below) Swarthmore College, which was named after the residence of George Fox. For the opening ceremonies of the college in October of 1869, Lucretia brought two young oak trees to be planted in her husband's honor. Courtesy of the Friends Historical Library of Swarthmore College

A photograph taken of Lucretia in 1879, the year before she died (*right*). Her determined gaze is more evident in the sculpture that memorializes her (*below*). The sculpture by Adelaide Johnson features Elizabeth Cady Stanton and Susan B. Anthony in addition to Lucretia. It was presented to the U.S. government in 1921 by the National Women's Party, and is now in the crypt of the U.S. Capitol.
Photograph of Lucretia by F. Gutekunst, 712 Arch St., Philadelphia; supplied courtesy of the Sophia Smith Collection, Smith College; photograph of the sculpture supplied courtesy of the Architect of the Capitol

Once inside the hall, the women were taken to special seats, where they met three other Quaker women. The six of them "prepared to sit quietly and listen." Apparently they did not consider challenging "the assumed superiority of the men" to conduct business. As biographer Margaret Hope Bacon writes, "It had not occurred to any of them, not even to Lucretia Mott, with her advanced views of women's rights, that women should actually participate in the deliberations." Yet the constitution of the society stated that "the privilege of membership [should be] conferred upon any person, not a slaveholder, who paid the dues of the association." Another historian wrote, "[Clearly], women were not regarded as 'persons.'"

Although Lucretia remained perfectly still in her seat, her eyes scanned the room repeatedly. There were sixty delegates assembled — several from Pennsylvania, as well as others from Massachusetts, Rhode Island, New York, New Jersey, and Delaware. Some, like James Mott, were older and more experienced in the work of social reform. Others, like Miller McKim, the 23-year-old theology student from Cumberland County, Pennsylvania, were fledglings in the anti-slavery arena. (Fledgling or not, Miller McKim was to become a good friend of Lucretia's. In a way, she became his mentor, and since both of them loved a good debate, they had spirited discussions with each other — both face to face and in letters.)

The sharp rap of chairman Beriah Green's gavel signaled the beginning of the meeting. The delegates proceeded to debate their first order of business: the drafting of the Declaration of Sentiments. This document, which stated the purpose, philosophy, and goals of the newly formed society, contained "a pledge to struggle not only against slavery, but also against prejudice, and to use only moral means in the fight."

Lucretia agreed wholeheartedly with the ideas put forth in the first draft of the declaration, but she objected to the wording of certain sections. In her years as a teacher, she had developed a sharp ear for grammatical correctness and proper sentence structure, skills that had been strengthened through her avid reading of British and American literature.

When the general secretary asked for the group's approval of the initial draft, Lucretia suddenly "found herself on her feet, asking permission . . . to say a few words." In more modern times, this would seem like a perfectly natural thing to do. But in the nineteenth century, "it was unheard of for a woman to speak in public." Benches creaked as "startled" male delegates turned to stare at the woman who "was violating a rigid rule of polite society." When Chairman Green had recovered from his initial surprise, he granted Lucretia permission to speak. "And I hope the lady will not hesitate to say all she is moved to during the course of the proceedings," he added.

Encouraged by his receptiveness, Lucretia politely suggested changes in the document's wording: "I suggest that in the sentence thou has just read . . . [it] will give a better climax if the two phrases are transposed." After speaking, she sat down again between her mother and daughter, her heart pounding rapidly in her chest. To address members of her own Quaker Meeting was one thing, but to comment on a precedent-setting reform document produced by a group of the most progressive thinkers in the nation was quite another. Still, a short while later she rose to correct another error.

It was largely because of the progressive attitudes of many of the delegates that Lucretia's suggestions were taken seriously. Chairman Green, William Lloyd Garrison, John Greenleaf Whittier, and others encouraged her continued participation. In his notes from the convention, Whittier, who acted as the secretary, wrote, "[Lucretia Mott was] a beautiful and graceful woman, with a clear, sweet voice. . . . She sat among us, quietly listening [and] occasionally giving . . . her thoughts on some point under discussion."

Lucretia, often accompanied by her mother and daughter, attended most of the week's meetings. On the final day, Chairman Green announced that several prominent abolitionists had refused to sign the new document. The politically aggressive plans of the newly formed society (members planned to distribute pamphlets, hire professional lecturers, and organize local societies in as many towns as possible) had apparently scared them off. According to Chairman Green, the men were afraid that if they signed the Declaration of Sentiments, their businesses would suffer and they would lose important friendships.

Lucretia found their lack of commitment appalling. Once again, she was on her feet, addressing the group, pointing out that "right principles were stronger than great names": "If our principles are right, . . . why should we wait for those who never had the courage to maintain the inalienable rights of the slave?"

Her impassioned remark was enough to convince several delegates who were hesitant about signing to step forward and add their names. Still, some delegates wavered. "It would be best to think it over," she heard one of the older ones whisper to James Mott. Lucretia, fearing that her husband might also hesitate, spoke up once again: "James, put down thy name!" As James stepped forward to sign, "a flicker of a smile at his indignant wife" spread across his face.

Public reaction to the convention was predictably disapproving. The *Philadelphia Inquirer* called the delegates "a collection of visionary fanatics." When word got out that "a woman [had appeared] in public," it caused "almost as much astonishment as the [anti-slavery] resolutions themselves."

On the heels of her small yet significant contribution to the first American Anti-Slavery Convention, Lucretia redoubled her efforts on behalf of slaves. She organized the Philadelphia Female Anti-Slavery Society (primarily patterned after the local all-male society) and helped to draft its constitution. Not surprisingly, the female group, like the male group, was integrated: a number of prominent black women became members. This "amalgamation," as it was called in the nineteenth century, troubled many in the city. As Margaret Hope Bacon explains, "These black women were all middle class and thoroughly respectable. Nevertheless, the mere fact that they were holding regular meetings with white women was enough to send shock waves through Philadelphia's body politic. From its moment of birth the little society of female abolitionists was suspect."

Lucretia and the other members were undaunted by public opinion. Lucretia developed friendships with the black women and invited them to her home. And the group, because of its makeup, became very involved in the black community in Philadelphia. It "developed an early welfare system," began working with black schools, and became increasingly involved in government petitions and public protests of injustices.

In addition, the society established an annual fair which, though frowned upon by conservative Quakers, raised significant amounts of money. The society used the money to publish anti-slavery literature, buy school supplies for the children of free blacks, and pay for the expenses of those traveling and lecturing for the cause of abolition.

As Lucretia became increasingly devoted to the anti-slavery movement and began speaking about slavery more and more in her work as a Quaker minister, the Quakers' negative sentiments against her rose. In general, both Hicksite and Orthodox members objected to the issue being discussed in Meeting. They pleaded with her "not to lug in the subject of slavery all the time." When she refused to oblige, "meetinghouses were refused her." The elders warned her to "keep in the quiet" and to "avoid all contentions."

In response, Lucretia "became increasingly critical of modern Quakerism." Her involvement with the women's anti-slavery group made her more and more aware of the inequities that still existed in the Society of Friends. For example, the Women's Meeting could discipline one of its members for what it considered misbehavior, but it was up to the men to decide whether or not to disown the offender. Why couldn't the women make this decision as well?

Clearly, Lucretia Mott was on her way to becoming a champion of the rights of many.

As time went on and circumstances changed, Philadelphia's attitude toward slavery became more ambiguous. A bustling port city just forty miles north of the Mason-Dixon line (an imaginary line dividing North and South), Philadelphia "was the first port-of-call" for cotton ships laden with the harvest from southern plantations. As the city expanded and modernized, it became a favorite vacation destination for wealthy Southerners, many of whom sent their sons to its fine medical schools. Many elected officials became "anxious not to disturb this profitable trade with the South . . . [and, consequently,] were increasingly pro-slavery." The politicians had the support of thousands of Philadelphia's middle-class citizens. Merchants and businessmen "depended on trade with the South; white workingmen . . . competed for jobs with the city's large Black population."

As a result of the increase in pro-slavery thinking in Philadelphia and other northern cities, leading abolitionists and their sympathizers became the objects of physical violence. Prudence Crandall, a New England schoolteacher who had established a school for black girls, was one such victim. In 1834, when she was attempting to open the school, an angry pro-slavery group had set fire to her Connecticut home and poisoned her drinking water, hoping to discourage her efforts.

But Prudence was not so easily deterred. Believing that Philadelphia might provide "a more congenial climate," she made plans to open a school there instead. For a week, she and her husband stayed with the Motts, who introduced her to several of the city's prominent black families. Lucretia then accompanied her into the poorer black neighborhoods to recruit students. "Prudence Crandall and her husband have passed a week in our city," Lucretia wrote to a friend. "She and myself called . . . on about 50 families . . . and engaged a sufficient number to warrant her beginning here — but there was so much opposition to the attempt, at this time . . . that she was induced to return to [New England]."

Meanwhile, violent anti-black riots were breaking

out in both New York City and Philadelphia and their suburbs. Groups of hostile whites burned black churches and vandalized black homes and businesses. Residents near the border of black and white neighborhoods lived "in an atmosphere of [constant] fear." Unfortunately, the police, among whom there were many pro-slavery supporters, did little to discourage conflicts. They were often late to arrive at riot scenes, then offered "half-hearted intervention."

The threat of violence weakened the resolve of many abolitionists. Some withdrew their support altogether, and though they were not won over to the pro-slavery side, they made it clear that they no longer wanted to be involved.

Lucretia showed no outward signs that the aggression displayed by pro-slavery supporters bothered her. She continued to host abolitionist meetings in her home, to organize fund-raisers on behalf of the city's poor blacks, and to distribute anti-slavery literature. And, despite warnings from her own Quaker colleagues, she continued to preach on the issue during Meeting.

Yet, while she remained outwardly composed, she was inwardly distressed. She lost weight, had trouble sleeping, and developed a stomach disorder that often caused her great pain. "The sheer stress of battle soon began to take a toll," explains biographer Margaret Hope Bacon. James, accustomed to seeing his vivacious wife effortlessly juggle her public and private responsibilities, was alarmed. He asked a family friend, Dr. Joseph Parrish, to examine Lucretia and recommend treatment.

Parrish based his diagnosis partly on accepted medical practices and partly on his own common sense. He told Lucretia that her ability to digest coffee and spicy and fatty foods (which she loved) had declined with age. He recommended changing to a blander diet consisting mainly of red meat with no gravy, dry bread, and plenty of chamomile tea. An additional cause of the stomach ailment, Parrish concluded, was most certainly prolonged periods of stress. "Thou art going too far too fast," he told her. "[Thou should] dissipate a little . . . indulge in more pleasure and relaxation."

At her husband's urging, Lucretia followed Parrish's diet for several weeks. But after finding it distasteful and somewhat ineffective, she abandoned it altogether. Despite the frequent stomach pains they gave her, she returned to her favorite foods: cornbread with butter, pickled herring, oysters, and blackberry pie.

As for "relaxation," Lucretia knew only how to work. "[She] could rarely fold her hands in idleness," wrote her granddaughter. She refused to cut back on her reform activities or her Quaker ministry. When Parrish, on a return visit, accused her of "running on nervous energy," she offered him a compromise: if he could find her an equal replacement in the anti-slavery crusade, then she would quit. Predictably, Parrish did not oblige and remained frustrated by Lucretia's "stoic" attitude toward her health problems.

In 1837 the Motts moved again, this time to a larger house on Ninth Street. Their new home had a dining room "big enough to seat fifty, and . . . enough bedrooms to house the basic family of eight or ten plus any number of out-of-town guests." During the warmer months, when travel from city to city was easier, abolitionists from Boston, New York, and New Jersey arrived frequently at the Mott house. "Reformers moved about the home almost as freely as the family itself," wrote one relative. "Even the transient visitor became immediately at home as he enjoyed a sense of his own worthiness, a feeling that he was an indispensable link in the chain." James was doing reasonably well in the wool business, but Lucretia had to employ all her skills of thrift to afford all the entertaining she did.

The year marked another milestone for Lucretia in what would eventually become a sixty-year history of activity in social reform. In May of 1837, she and her oldest daughter, Anna Hopper, led a delegation of seventeen to New York City for the First Annual Anti-Slavery Convention of American Women, which Lucretia had organized with Maria Chapman, the leader of the women's anti-slavery group in Boston. In the four short years that the Philadelphia group had been in existence, its members had become more self-assured, and their membership had grown steadily. Under Lucretia's leadership, they had run dozens of meetings, corresponded regularly with other women's groups, organized fund-raising events, and voiced their opinions on social issues.

The three-day convention gave the Philadelphia delegates an opportunity to meet and exchange ideas with dozens of other delegates who were dedicated to abolition. Some of these women, like Angelina and Sarah Grimké, were already widely known in other parts of the country. The Grimkés had been born and raised on a southern plantation, and were converted to the abolitionist cause after witnessing the repeated mistreatment of slaves. Sarah Grimké remembered being only five when she saw a slave girl being beaten, and she "had never forgotten the sight."

Free-thinking and philosophical, the Grimkés had abandoned their southern roots, moved to Philadelphia, and joined the Society of Friends. In March of 1835, Angelina had been so moved by a speech she heard by a British abolitionist that she joined the Female Anti-Slavery Society. That summer, when violence against the abolitionists escalated in Philadelphia, Angelina wrote a personal letter to William Lloyd Garrison urging him never to abandon the cause. Without seeking Angelina's permission, Garrison printed the letter in his newspaper, the *Liberator*. Angelina was immediately popular; the eloquence of her letter prompted more and more calls for her to speak. In response, she began lecturing locally to groups of women meeting in private homes.

In 1836 both she and her sister wrote impassioned anti-slavery pamphlets: Angelina wrote *An Appeal to the Christian Women of the South,* and Sarah wrote *An Epistle to the Clergy of the Southern States.* That same year the sisters moved to New York and began addressing larger groups. In fact, they became such popular speakers that men began "infiltrating" their primarily female audiences.

This habit of speaking to "promiscuous audiences" (groups composed of both men and women) was the principal reason that the Grimké sisters became a controversial pair. In the nineteenth century, it was perfectly acceptable for men to address such groups, but decidedly unacceptable for women to do so. But at the First Anti-Slavery Convention of American Women, the Grimké sisters received strong support for their bold activities.

Bolstered by this encouragement, the sisters set off on a speaking tour through New England. They were considered "[among] the most controversial and exotic of anti-slavery agents." Their appearance before a mixed audience in Lynn, Massachusetts, sparked an angry response. "Their . . . behavior drew the wrath of the Massachusetts clergy, who denounced them for assuming 'the place and tone of man as public reformer,'" writes historian Nancy Woloch. The New England ministers, who carefully guarded the power they wielded in their communities, declared that "such activism was unnatural. . . . By describing the victimization of slave women, the Grimkes lost 'that modesty and delicacy . . . which constitutes the true influence of women in society.'"

The Massachusetts clergymen were not the first to try to prevent women from entering intellectual circles, preferring that they remain narrowly confined to their roles as wives and mothers. But the time had come for change. As Sarah Grimké stated in her *Letters on the Condition of Women and the Equality of the Sexes,* it was time for women to claim their rights as "equal . . . moral and accountable beings." "All I ask," she wrote, "[is that] our brethren . . . take their feet from off our necks and permit us to stand upright on the ground which God destined for us to occupy."

In the work of the Grimké sisters, Lucretia recognized a philosophy which echoed that of Mary Wollstonecraft, whose early treatise on women's rights had shaped her own views on gender equality. It did not take her long to realize that the condition of women and that of the slave were related, and that securing equal rights for one group would necessitate demanding them for the other.

But many abolitionists did not share this conviction. In the years that followed, "the woman question," more than any other single issue, affected the course of the anti-slavery movement. As more and more women became involved in social reforms, gaining confidence in their own abilities, women's rights and abolition became powerfully linked. "We have good cause to be grateful to the slave," said Abby Kelley, who later became a prominent abolitionist. "In striving to take his irons off, we found most surely that we were [chained] ourselves."

CHAPTER 8

Speaking Out for Freedom

As women became more involved in the anti-slavery movement, public sentiment against them increased. Many pro-slavery individuals opposed equal rights for blacks *and* women and felt justified in condemning both. In Massachusetts, a group of Protestant ministers issued a public statement declaring, "When [Woman] assumes the place of Man as public reformer, she yields the power which God has given her for her protection, and her character becomes unnatural. If the vine, whose strength and beauty is to lean upon the trellis-work, thinks to assume the independence of the elm, it will not only cease to bear fruit, but fall in shame and dishonor to the dust."

Throughout the 1830s, the slavery issue was at the root of many violent conflicts. In Philadelphia and other northern cities, pro-slavery groups participated in riots, vandalism, and even murder. In a letter to her young friend Miller McKim, Lucretia wrote, "The late outrages in this and other places were . . . shameful. . . . [But they have] aroused the indignation of friends of the people of colour in the surrounding country. . . . [Thus] we have reason to believe that all these things . . . altho meant for evil may be turned to good."

In May of 1838, the Second Anti-Slavery Convention of American Women was held in Philadelphia. Delegates from major cities in the North gathered inside Pennsylvania Hall, the new abolitionist center on North Sixth Street. The Motts had helped to raise thousands of dollars toward its construction, which had been completed that spring. "No efforts had been spared," wrote one abolitionist, "to make [it] an ornament to the city as well as a solid, sturdy edifice, consisting of several ground floor rooms, suitable for offices and small conferences, and a main auditorium offering space for about three thousand persons."

As the delegates entered the hall on the first day, they passed an angry pro-slavery mob gathered outside. Besides protesting abolition, most of them objected to Lucretia's intention to address "amalgamated" (racially mixed) audiences. The women's anti-slavery group had an additional problem: they couldn't decide among themselves whether or not women should be allowed to speak to "promiscuous" audiences (groups of men and women). Nevertheless, the convention moved forward. There were stirring speeches by William Lloyd Garrison, Angelina Grimké Weld, young Abby Kelley (who was to become a prominent abolitionist), and, of course, Lucretia Mott. Meanwhile, tensions on the street continued to rise. The dedication ceremonies for the hall had begun on Monday, May 14; by Wednesday, the size and the discontent of the mob were growing; by Thursday, the mob was "huge and ugly." The president of the hall, Daniel Neall, asked the mayor for protection; he was simply told that the unrest was the abolitionists' own fault, and that the best thing to do would be to keep black women from attending the meetings. Lucretia was the one who reported that message to the conference Thursday afternoon "but said that she did not agree with it and that she hoped none of the women would be put off 'by a little appearance of danger.' Then she arranged for the women to leave the hall two by two, a white woman in arm with a black one."

But by evening the mob was seventeen thousand strong, and the danger finally exploded into violence. Although the mayor locked the doors to the hall and told the crowd that he was shutting down the conference, he made only a mild plea for peace and then left, without providing any protection for the hall. The mob simply broke down the doors, piled the books and benches together, and set them on fire. The city firemen were called, but, like the police, they responded half-heartedly. "They directed their hoses only at neighboring buildings," one delegate reported.

Early the next morning, when the fire was nearly out, the mob began to search for new targets. Rumors circulated that abolitionists' homes, including the

Motts', would be next. Undeterred, James and Lucretia sent her mother and the younger children to a friend's house several blocks away, then returned late that afternoon to wait "for whatever the night might bring." Quaker friends "rushed in and urged them to flee, but [Lucretia] went on serving supper in her usual way." Their son Thomas "loitered near the front steps, listening for the mob."

As darkness fell, the assailants approached. Lucretia "stiffened, listening to the hideous yells" of the angry mob. "I was scarcely breathing," she recalled later, "but I felt willing to suffer whatever the cause required." Luckily, a close friend of the Motts intervened. Posing as a pro-slavery supporter, he joined the crowd, shouting, "On to the Motts!" and cleverly led them in the wrong direction. Eventually, the mob gave up the search, choosing instead to vandalize a black church and orphanage on Sixth Street.

The experience made Lucretia acutely aware of humankind's potential for violence, and she remained more determined than ever to promote peace among people of different races, genders, and religions. The next morning, she presided over the final meeting of the convention. As the damage to Pennsylvania Hall was being assessed, the women gathered in a schoolhouse on Cherry Street. Undaunted by ongoing threats, they voted unanimously to continue their annual conventions and produced the following declaration against racial prejudice:

Resolved, That prejudice against color is the very spirit of slavery. It is, therefore, the duty of abolitionists to identify themselves with these oppressed Americans, by sitting with them in places of worship, by appearing with them in our streets, by giving them our [respect] in steamboats and stages, by visiting them at their homes and encouraging them to visit us, receiving them as we do our white fellow citizens.

Although the convention ended on this strong note, Lucretia was somewhat depressed. The burning of Pennsylvania Hall had pained her, and she faced trials in her personal life too. For one thing, she felt no comfort "in or out of Meeting," and she couldn't imagine preaching again. In addition, James had lost a great deal of money when a company in which he had an interest burned down, so now they were poor again. But after several months she had "regained her usual good spirits."

The following spring, Lucretia had to hunt for a place to hold the third anti-slavery convention. All seven of the Friends groups in the downtown area refused her, as did all the churches — except the Universalist Church, which offered a space that wasn't nearly large enough. In the end the convention had to be held in a stable.

In the days preceding the convention, Philadelphia's Mayor Roach paid the Motts a visit. He implored Lucretia to "avoid 'unnecessary walking with colored people' [in order] to prevent the outrages that had occurred the previous year." Lucretia understood the mayor's concern, but it made her angry nonetheless. "[I have] been in the habit of walking with colored people," she told him firmly, "and [will] continue that practice. . . . [And] as [I] expect to have house guests 'of that complexion' [I will] in all probability be accompanying them to and from the convention."

Despite the mayor's concern, the meetings that year were "undisturbed." But "the woman question" continued to cause problems within the larger anti-slavery movement. Abolitionists who favored the inclusion of women argued constantly with those who opposed it.

In 1840, tensions reached their peak. William Lloyd Garrison, who supported the women's cause, convinced his followers to elect Lucretia and two other women — Lydia Marie Child and Maria Chapman — to the Anti-Slavery Society's national executive committee. Several prominent abolitionists who opposed the women's election split off to form an all-male anti-slavery group known as "The New Org." Lucretia was dismayed at the loss of these committed abolitionists. Although she sided with Garrison on "the woman question," she had encouraged him to be more diplomatic in his approach. "[I wish] that our dear and much-respected friend Garrison would record . . . the local dissensions and the details of divisions . . . more sparingly in his paper," she told a friend.

Lucretia's opinion of Garrison's methods extended to the issue of "nonresistance" as well. In theory, she supported the notion that physical force of any sort — whether within the context of family, community, workplace, or national defense — should rarely if ever be used. But she was not so sure that Garrison's rigid rejection "not only of force but all government based on force" was realistic for a young, multicultural nation like the United States.

Nonetheless, she continued to support Garrison by attending meetings of his newly formed New England Non-Resistance Society. The Quaker elders opposed her affiliation with Garrison, reminding her that even the most liberal Hicksite considered him a "radical."

This constant criticism wore Lucretia down. The very organization that had given her the freedom to become a leader now accused her of "mingling with 'the World's people'" and "substituting good causes for true religion." Nevertheless, Lucretia continued traveling as a minister, and she continued preaching about both abolition and nonresistance. The turmoil that this situation created took its toll: among other things, Lucretia's stomach problems flared up again.

But in the spring of 1840, Lucretia was chosen as a delegate to the first World's Anti-Slavery Convention, and that proved an effective antidote for her troubles. In London, she established her friendship with Elizabeth Cady Stanton, which would last the rest of her life, and she began to fully understand the extent to which women were denied full participation in public life. "After we had travelled over [to] England," she wrote in her diary, "we [realized] how far we considered [women's] minds fettered and crushed by public opinion and external restraints."

Despite the controversy surrounding the convention, Lucretia returned to the United States refreshed and renewed. Increasingly, she was regarded as a leader among abolitionists as well as a leading spokesperson for women's rights. "The [London] experience unleashed her," writes Margaret Hope Bacon; "thereafter she did not attempt to hold back either anger or commitment."

Her psychological rejuvenation coincided with a spiritual revival, and she devoted more time to her Quaker ministry. Her children were older now and more independent, allowing her increased freedom to travel to speak and preach. And she and James were becoming more financially comfortable again. Frequently accompanied by her husband, she traveled extensively throughout Pennsylvania and its neighboring states between 1840 and 1844. Citizens jammed meetinghouses in dozens of small towns to hear her preach and deliver anti-slavery speeches. She addressed the legislatures of Pennsylvania, New Jersey, and Delaware, arguing in favor of immediate abolition: "Bear with me when I speak for those who may not speak for themselves. . . . Righteousness exalteth a nation but [the] sin [of slavery] is a lasting reproach. Let us not hesitate to wipe [out] this disgrace — this foulest blot."

Although she found support for abolition in many of the towns she visited, she was not afraid to travel into pro-slavery territory. When she arrived in Smyrna, Delaware (a slave state), in 1841, she was greeted suspiciously by its citizens. It was a cold First Day (Sunday) in February, and both Quakers and non-Quakers alike were gathered at the local meetinghouse to hear her preach. There was tension in the air as the doors opened and the crowd filed in slowly and took their seats. Many wondered aloud if Mrs. Mott would "dare to mention slavery," and what the effect would be if she did.

Lucretia sat facing them on a wooden bench, nervously adjusting her bonnet and smoothing the wrinkles in her plain gray dress. She looked up briefly and found James, seated in the back, nodding his head in encouragement. Several silent moments passed. Finally, she rose and began her sermon. She kept her message general at first, emphasizing the need for all people to obey God's natural laws and be committed to his will. Gradually, however, she turned the topic to slavery. "There was a sharp intake of breaths," recalled one observer, and a man seated in the front of the room "rose and angrily stalked [out]." But the rest stayed to listen, and Lucretia concluded her sermon "without a disturbance."

However, upon returning to their carriage, James and Lucretia found it vandalized. Lucretia gladly accepted a Friend's offer to fix the vehicle, and prepared to wait with James at a nearby inn while the job was completed. But the innkeeper, a pro-slavery sympathizer, stood in their way. "There's too much excitement," he said, and shut the door in their faces. The Motts had not been invited to any of the homes in Smyrna, and so they were forced to wait outside in the freezing darkness.

The carriage took more than an hour to repair. Now thoroughly chilled and hungry, the Motts thanked the repairman and huddled close together on the wooden carriage seat, bracing themselves for the long drive to the next town.

Lucretia was disappointed but undaunted by such experiences. In the fall of 1842, she decided to venture further south, into the slave state of Virginia. With James along for company and moral support, she held seventeen meetings in eighteen days, preaching in towns such as Winchester, Alexandria, Harper's Ferry, and Frederickstown. In a letter to friends in Philadelphia, James wrote, "All of them were well-attended . . . but some elderly Friends were fearful lest we might cause an excitement and wanted the subject of slavery let alone . . . but the younger Friends and common people heard [Lucretia] gladly and acknowledged the truth of what was said."

After their tour of Virginia, the Motts proceeded to Washington, D.C. Since Lucretia wasn't able to get a hearing in the House of Representatives, James wrote to John Quincy Adams (who had served as U.S. President from 1825 to 1829) to ask if his wife could speak in Congressional Hall. Adams supported her request, but others did not. After further consideration, she was told that she could use the Hall if she "promised not to mention slavery."

Lucretia could not accept this restriction and chose instead to hold the gathering at a nearby Unitarian church in early January 1843. "Lucretia Mott from Philadelphia will attend Friends' Meeting in this city on Sunday morning next at 11 o'clock and [will speak] at the Unitarian Church at 7 in the evening," the local papers announced.

When Sunday night arrived, people poured into the church, "filling it to overflowing." The audience included more than forty Congressmen and the eminent writer/philosopher Ralph Waldo Emerson. Lucretia spoke for more than two hours, addressing such controversial issues as the unjust subordination of women, religious intolerance, racial prejudice, and the institution of slavery. Appealing to the Christlike goodness that she believed every listener possessed, she challenged all present to take action against the social evils of the day:

> I believe it to be high time there was more Christian boldness, more moral courage, amongst mankind to speak to the sentiment of their hearts, whether they be in accordance with the popular doctrines of the day or not. . . . Did not Jesus Christ come immediately in contact with forms and customs of that day? . . . It was his mission to break down these forms and ceremonies

and institute a practical religion. . . . He was almost daily brought up before the [leaders] of his day for offenses against their laws and regulations. . . . It would be well for us to compare this with the institutions of our day, and see whether the effect would be the same, were anyone to rise up in the present age against prevailing practices. . . . I cannot but look forward to that time when we shall understand the true character of righteousness, and shall bring the great principles of Christianity to bear upon the conduct of our everyday life.

Those in the audience were visibly moved and deeply impressed. Many, including Emerson himself, praised Lucretia for her courage in tackling volatile issues. "The sensation that attended the speech was like the rumble of an earthquake," Emerson wrote to his wife. "No man could have said so much and come away alive."

Riding the groundswell of support that followed, Lucretia set her sights on the White House. She and James managed to meet with President John Tyler, a slave-owner, who supported colonization as the solution to the slavery problem. Lucretia firmly articulated her support for abolition and allowing slaves to live where they chose. Although Lucretia did not succeed in persuading Tyler to change his views, he later admitted to admiring her "sturdy character" and being "charmed" by her eloquent presentation.

Lucretia left Washington feeling frustrated but not defeated. "Our hopes," she concluded, "must not rest on those in power, but on the common people . . . [and] their unprejudiced hearts."

After the Motts returned to Philadelphia, they had an important guest: Ralph Waldo Emerson. "Lucretia Mott . . . is beautiful to me," Emerson wrote in a letter to his wife. "She is a . . . genius of her church. . . . I do not wonder that [the Friends] are too proud of her and too much in awe of her to spare her, though they suspect her faith."

Emerson's assessment of Lucretia's situation was accurate. After news spread of Lucretia's "successful public speech in a Unitarian church," she was opposed and criticized more frequently in Philadelphia. At the Philadelphia Yearly Meeting in the spring of 1843, another female minister spoke against her for more than an hour. In October of that year, George White, a New York minister known for his strong opposition to abolitionists, came to Philadelphia and preached against reform at Lucretia's own Cherry Street Meeting. And in that same month, she was disciplined by the Society: she would no longer be given traveling minutes (formal letters of introduction), which had helped smooth the way for her as a traveling preacher.

It was trials like these that made Lucretia wonder if she should renounce her membership in the Society of Friends. But if she did so, she would "leave the Society she loved in the hands of the conservatives"; she would also lose her privilege to speak in Meeting, which she always enjoyed. So Lucretia persevered despite the disapproval and discipline she faced. She continued to travel and preach against slavery. But she paid a high price for her perseverance. As Margaret Hope Bacon points out, "She was frequently received coldly, ordered to sit down, and sometimes turned away."

During this difficult time, Lucretia relied, as she always did, on the support of family and friends. Particularly important to her was her mother's support. Sadly, this was something that she would soon lose.

CHAPTER 9

Birth of a Revolution

Early in the spring of 1844, both Lucretia and her mother, Anna Coffin, contracted influenza. This disease frequently reached epidemic proportions in the nineteenth century, and it was not uncommon for families to lose several of their members at once.

Lucretia's children provided constant care for the two women, whose vitality, industry, and spiritual strength had sustained the family through good and bad times. James undertook the delicate task of politely refusing the dozens of well-meaning visitors who came to the house inquiring about Lucretia's condition. He could only stand helplessly by as his wife lay sick in bed, considerably weakened by bouts of "fever, vomiting, and congestion of the lungs." Lucretia's concern for her mother took precedence over her own health, however, and she refused to rest. Finally she convinced James to "wrap her up in a blanket and carry her to her mother's bed." Finding Anna "much worse" than she had expected, Lucretia became "very upset" and had to return to her room to recover.

Lucretia's mother was clearly losing the fight. Influenza was particularly hard on the very young and the very old, and seventy-three-year-old Anna weakened steadily. Toward the end of March she fell into a coma from which she never awoke. She died in Lucretia's house on March 26, 1844.

The shock was almost too much for Lucretia to bear. Already physically weakened by her illness, she was now emotionally devastated by her mother's death. As a consequence, she contracted encephalitis (an inflammation of the brain) and was considered in critical condition for several days. Dr. Parrish's son, who had taken over since his father's retirement, was called in immediately to treat her. Young Parrish tried all of the accepted remedies of the day, including "leeches, mustard plasters and castor oil."

As Lucretia fought for her life, her children sent for their Aunt Martha, who lived in Auburn, New York. Martha hurried to Philadelphia, and her arrival proved to be the turning point in her sister's illness. As Lucretia improved, the family remained vigilant, insisting — despite Lucretia's protests — that she remain in bed and follow the doctor's advice.

By the end of April, Lucretia was gaining back much of her former strength. She began "demanding all the political news she had missed." Her abolitionist friends came to visit, but James cautioned them not to burden her with pressing problems until she was completely well.

By summertime, Lucretia was physically recovered. Yet she remained emotionally shaken by the loss of her mother and her own brush with death. For the next two-and-a-half years, she remained close to home most of the time, appeared less frequently in public, and was content to spend time with family members and close friends. Her deep respect for the natural cycles of life — growth and recovery, loss and renewal, rest and work — became apparent at this time. She understood intuitively the need to withdraw and to regroup her physical, spiritual, and emotional forces.

Still, Lucretia was far from inactive during this time. By the fall, she became involved in developing the Association for the Relief of Poor Women. This became an important organization in Philadelphia, for as the city expanded, the number of poor people rapidly increased. The sponsors of the association used the money they raised to rent a room in which poor women could get together to sew items ordered by those who were more financially comfortable. Not surprisingly, Lucretia was elected president of the association.

During the summer of 1845, she and James traveled to the Ohio Yearly Meeting in Salem, near Pittsburgh. There Lucretia preached on the topic of women's rights. This was a significant event — later called "the first such speech by a woman, for women, in the Midwest."

In the fall of 1846, Lucretia ruffled some Quaker

feathers again. It all started innocently enough. Her sister Martha came for a visit, and the two of them decided "on the spur of the moment" to attend the convention that the local Unitarian Church was holding. As it turned out, Lucretia was asked to speak, and she couldn't say no. When the Philadelphia papers published her comments, some Unitarians were offended that a woman had spoken in their church, but the Quakers were enraged that one of their "flock" had spoken to outsiders as a representative of the Society. Lucretia hadn't made this claim, but she had been introduced this way when she spoke. The result was another visit to Philadelphia by George White, and another attack on Lucretia.

That winter Lucretia again turned her attention to the increasing problem of poverty in Philadelphia. Among other things, both she and James helped workers who were striking for better wages.

By the spring of 1847, Lucretia was "her old self again." She was eager to continue her ministry, so she and James left Philadelphia and journeyed west by stage, steamboat, and train to Ohio. There, during a series of anti-slavery meetings, Lucretia addressed as many as five thousand people. Among them were William Lloyd Garrison and Frederick Douglass, the latter noting that he "had never seen Mrs. Mott under more favorable circumstances." In the abolitionist journal *The Anti-Slavery Standard,* Douglass wrote, "Her silvery voice is distinctly heard . . . [and] her truthful words

119

came down upon the audience like drops of summer rain."

But Lucretia was not welcomed and praised wherever she went. Many Quakers resented her anti-slavery views, and others questioned her allegiance to the Society. Because of this, she was sometimes treated unkindly. That fall, for example, during the Yearly Meeting of Friends in Richmond, Indiana, Lucretia and James were forced to stay in a lodging house because none of the local Quakers had offered them hospitality. When the Motts began attending the sessions, Lucretia was treated so coldly that she developed severe leg pains that kept her off her feet for several days. When James tried to get a local Quaker doctor to treat Lucretia, the doctor refused on the grounds that Lucretia's behavior bothered him too much. Although this incident "reduced her to tears," Lucretia recovered in time to return to the sessions. Despite her poor health, she "felt it was her duty to endure the ostracism . . . in order to remind [the other participants] of their duty to the slave and of the simple Quakerism of an earlier day."

In fact, in January of 1848, Lucretia added fuel to the fire by agreeing, along with her husband James, to allow William Lloyd Garrison to use her name as one of the supporters of his proposed Anti-Sabbath Convention. Garrison and his followers "questioned the current strict observance of the Sabbath, which in their view deprived workingmen of any recreation on their one day of rest and made it unacceptable to pursue any reform activities." Lucretia supported the spirit of this query whole-heartedly. (Years ago she had stopped going to afternoon Meeting and spent the time "visiting black families or poor women" instead.) And she not only attended the convention but also spoke several times. So once again Lucretia became a target of Friends' outrage. This time she was labeled one of the "spouters of heresy." Nevertheless, Lucretia was determined to remain a Quaker *and* support the causes and the individuals she believed in.

The following June, the Motts visited the Seneca Indian reservation in northern New York. (They were members of that state's Indian Committee.) Upon their arrival, Lucretia was dismayed at the condition of the dwindling tribe. It had lost many of its members to a recent epidemic of typhus, and Lucretia observed that "the remaining few hundred . . . were suffering . . . from poverty and discord." The discord was a result of recent efforts at evangelism: "Several missionaries had been visiting the reservation and making converts," according to biographer Margaret Hope Bacon, "with the result there was now a Christian and a Pagan party." While James mingled with the men and assisted with repairs to their homes and farm buildings, Lucretia tried to help by meeting with representatives of both parties and listening to their complaints. She did not preach to them about Quakerism. She had seen the Senecas' sacred Strawberry Dance, and it had opened her eyes to "the deep religious fervor" of the people.

On their way home, James and Lucretia visited Martha Wright and her family in Auburn. Elizabeth Cady Stanton, who had recently moved from the bustling intellectual center of Boston to the tiny, rustic town of Seneca Falls, heard of their arrival and eagerly accepted an invitation to tea. Lucretia was delighted at the opportunity to renew her friendship with Stanton (they had met in 1840 at the World's Anti-Slavery Convention), and she soon found herself immersed in a lively discussion of women's rights.

In the eight years since their initial meeting in London, Stanton's interest in the subject had grown. As the daughter of a prominent Boston lawyer and the wife of abolitionist Henry Stanton, she was well versed in the workings of both law and politics. Like Lucretia, she was an avid reader and referred frequently to the feminist writings of Mary Wollstonecraft, Lydia Maria Child (a popular Boston writer and editor of *The National Anti-Slavery Standard*), and Angelina Grimké.

But it was Stanton's personal experience as a daughter, wife, and mother that had served to solidify her impassioned support for gender equality. As a young girl, she had seen battered women come to her father's office, pleading for some legal protection. When Daniel Cady had explained that this was impossible (in fact, laws existed that gave husbands the right to hit their wives) and lent his support to laws that kept women powerless, Elizabeth began to question his principles. She had felt that powerlessness herself when, as a young woman on her honeymoon in London, she had attended the World's Anti-Slavery Convention: she had been forced to sit with the rest of the women in the balcony and had been denied participation in the meetings. She had since become the mother of three boys (she would have four more children in the next several years), and with Henry frequently away, the responsibilities of the household "rested [squarely] on her shoulders."

Not surprisingly, the vivacious and intellectually oriented Elizabeth found full-time housekeeping and motherhood "depressing." As she wrestled with feelings of guilt, anger, resentment, and helplessness, she wondered if other women experienced the same kind of frustration. "I keep the house and grounds in good order, the wardrobes in proper trim, take the boys to the dentists, shoemakers, schools," she told Lucretia and Martha wearily. "I sew all . . . those ruffles on our pillowcases and nightcaps [and] on the shirts we make for our lords."

On the afternoon of July 13, 1848, the three of them met for tea at the home of Jane Hunt, a local Hicksite Friend. Mary Ann McClintock, another Hicksite and "a relative of Jane's by marriage," was also present. The discussion centered once again on the subject of women's rights. One by one the women listed the grievances most often heard from their female friends and family members: precious hours lost to repetitive household tasks, struggles with boredom, social isolation, and lack of educational and professional opportunities. If these problems were as widespread as they seemed, asked Stanton, would it not be appropriate to hold a convention to publicly proclaim their views and elicit support? The other women readily agreed, and before the afternoon was over, they had placed a notice in the *Seneca County Courier*:

> WOMAN'S RIGHTS CONVENTION: A Convention to discuss the social, civil, and religious conditions and rights of woman, will be held in the Wesleyan Chapel at Seneca Falls, N.Y., on Wednesday and Thursday, the 19th and 20th of July current, commencing at 10 o'clock A.M. During the first day the meeting will be exclusively for women, who are earnestly invited to attend. The public generally are invited to be present on the second day when Lucretia Mott, of Philadelphia, and other ladies and gentlemen, will address the Convention.

On July 14, the five met again at Mary McClintock's home to "prepare a program." Brimming with enthusiasm, the women nonetheless struggled to create an acceptable format for their Declaration of Sentiments, which would summarize the philosophy and goals of the group. "How could the grievances of eleven million women be compressed into a few telling lines?" they wondered. At last, while "searching through the McClintocks' bookcase," Stanton came upon a copy of the Declaration of Independence. She read it aloud, changing "a phrase here and there":

> We hold these truths to be self-evident: that all men and *women* are created equal; that they are endowed by their Creator with certain inalienable rights; that among these are life, liberty, and the pursuit of happiness. . . . The history of Mankind is a history of repeated injuries and usurpations on the part of man toward woman, . . . [resulting in] the establishment of an absolute tyranny over her. To prove this, let facts [now] be submitted. . . .

Pleased with their progress and the power of this amended declaration, the women adjourned until the following Wednesday.

When Lucretia and James approached Wesleyan Chapel on July 19, they saw "several dozen men and women standing outside." After learning that the minister had left town with the key, they hoisted Elizabeth's nephew through the window and opened the doors from the inside. Within the next half hour, nearly three hundred curious citizens arrived, far more than any of the convention's creators had expected. Even more surprising was the number of men who wished to attend. After a brief discussion, Lucretia and Elizabeth decided to open the meetings on both days to everyone, even though they had initially set aside the first day for women alone.

But this decision created another problem. In non-Quaker circles, it was still socially unacceptable for a woman to preside over a "mixed gathering." To avoid unnecessary criticism, the women asked James Mott to open the meeting and introduce the speakers. He willingly agreed, and in his slow, dignified manner he called the assembly to order. He then invited his wife to the podium to make the first speech.

The room was silent. All eyes focused on "the little gray-gowned figure" as she explained "the necessity of inaugurating a progressive movement aimed to raise woman from her degrading position [and to overcome] the economic, social, and political wrongs which were imposed upon her." Lucretia was followed by her sister Martha Wright, who read the humorous sketch she had written in support of women's rights.

Elizabeth Stanton spoke next. Her voice wavered slightly as she made her first public speech and read the Declaration of Sentiments. Although the crowd included many liberal members of the New York Hicksites, they were clearly unprepared for such a thoroughly progressive document. Stanton, red-cheeked and trembling slightly, managed to maintain her poise throughout the first reading, gaining confidence during each subsequent review. "No official count of the number of times the 'Declaration' was read seems available," writes biographer Otelia Cromwell. "But the Minutes record that the document was not only read at each of the six sessions of the Convention, but was reread and discussed 'paragraph by paragraph' and after much consideration some changes were suggested and adopted."

Stanton seemed more at ease as she offered the eleven subsequent resolutions that the five women had listed at their informal meeting. Among these were the right of women to have equal educational opportunities, to secure the same legal rights as men regarding property ownership and child custody, and the removal of the social barriers that prevented women from entering professions such as law and medicine.

Lastly, Stanton placed before the mixed gathering a demand for women's "sacred right of elective franchise." This resolution was by far the most controversial. Even Lucretia, whose zealous support for women's rights had influenced her actions for the past three decades, had been hesitant to lend her support to that particular resolution. Although she agreed with Stanton in principle, her greater experience in social reforms had taught her that asking for too much change too quickly could, in the end, be harmful to the cause. "We must go slowly at first!" she had cautioned Elizabeth in a motherly tone.

But Stanton remained firm on the issue. She was convinced that "on the principle [of suffrage] the future of the [women's] cause was doomed to success or failure." Former slave and respected abolitionist Frederick Douglass supported Stanton's position. On the second day of the convention, he spoke out in favor of the controversial resolution, declaring that "the right of suffrage [is] the first step toward complete freedom." Because of his strong endorsement, the resolution passed by a few votes (the other resolutions passed easily).

Exhausted from the proceedings but overjoyed by their apparent success, Stanton, Hunt, McClintock, and Wright asked Lucretia to say a few words. She agreed, and gave a passionate address that lasted for an hour. Emphasizing the need for sweeping social change, she called for an "overthrow of the monopoly of the pulpit and for the securing to women an equal participation with men in the various trades, professions and commerce."

The signing of the Declaration of Sentiments and the attached resolutions marked the end of the formal meetings. Lucretia was the first to sign, followed by sixty-seven women and thirty-two men.

The Seneca Falls convention was a success, so Lucretia and her friends were surprised that it created a "storm of criticism." According to Margaret Hope Bacon, "Almost every newspaper in the country carried an editorial attacking or ridiculing [the event]." Angry headlines appeared in major journals and newspapers: "INSURRECTION AMONG WOMEN," "SOCIALISM," "HEN CONVENTION." Reporters targeted Lucretia as the instigator of a new "revolution," portraying her as a power-hungry radical with a "dagger concealed under her clothes . . . [with intention to] involve us in all the horrors of anarchy and insurrection."

By now accustomed to public ridicule, Lucretia

chose to ignore these personal attacks. To underscore her commitment to the cause, she accepted an invitation to speak at a second women's rights convention just two weeks later. Held in a Unitarian church in Rochester, New York, this smaller meeting provided Lucretia with a truly intellectual audience. Several conservative clergymen who were in attendance wasted no time putting forth their arguments for the continued subordination of women. They reminded her that Saint Paul had said, "Man shall be the head of the woman." Was Mrs. Mott now proposing that Christians ignore the Scriptures? Lucretia responded with poise and tact. "Obedience" was absent from the Quakers' marriage vows, she told them, and she "had never seen any difficulty arising in the Society of Friends from [that] fact." Furthermore, she reminded them, Paul had advised against marriage altogether. Should all wives and husbands therefore be counted as sinners? This silenced the clergymen, who realized immediately that the speaker's knowledge of the Scriptures should not be questioned.

Lucretia fielded many other questions from the Rochester audience concerning women's "proper sphere" and their suitability for public life. Drawing on her own life experience, her biblical knowledge, and her scholarly readings, she applied logic, moral philosophy, and ethics to successfully counter arguments based on prejudice and superstition.

The women's rights movement, still in its infant

stages, gained momentum after Rochester. Ironically, public criticism of both conventions served only to bolster the cause. "The nationwide publicity aroused women everywhere," writes biographer Dorothy Sterling. "Before long, women's Equal Rights Unions and Equal Suffrage Societies were springing up all over the North and West."

But not all women supported gender equality. Many were influenced by the popular argument that women were by nature intellectually inferior to men and therefore unfit for the rigors of higher education, the professions, or any sort of public life. "They have learned to hug their chains!" Lucretia said of those women who feared the challenges of gaining social, political, and economic equality.

Others were swayed by religious arguments put forth by priests and ministers. These men used specific passages in the Bible to support the concept of male superiority, while ignoring other passages that argued just as strongly for equal rights.

Despite the difficulty of changing both men's *and* women's opinions, Lucretia remained determined to champion her cause.

In 1849 the cycle of renewal and loss once again played through Lucretia's life. Two more grandchildren (she now had ten) were born in January and March. But by that summer Philadelphia was in the throes of a cholera epidemic, and her brother Thomas Coffin succumbed to it. Once again Lucretia experienced "a deep and devastating sense of loss." She wrote very frankly about it to her sister Martha, and she kept herself busy with charitable activities: for several weeks that summer she opened her home to an English mother and her children "who were stranded in Philadelphia."

But this was also to be a year of triumph for Lucretia. In the fall of 1849 (by which time the epidemic was over), the prominent New England writer Richard Henry Dana delivered a series of lectures in Philadelphia. During one of these, entitled "An Address on Woman," Dana used passages from the Bible and examples from the writings of John Milton and William Shakespeare "to prove that women [are] physically, mentally, and morally weaker than men." Calling the recent surge of interest in gender equality "a threat to conventional society," Dana attacked the women's rights movement from every angle. Lucretia, who attended the lecture, was "appalled" by it; afterward she frankly told Dana that he had obviously been misled and was now misleading others. Bystanders recalled that Dana "blushed, sputtered, and turned away."

Lucretia thought it unfair that only one side of the argument was presented. Not surprisingly, "when several prominent Philadelphians asked her if she would reply to the attack, she was happy to say yes." In her "Discourse on Woman," which she delivered in Philadelphia on December 17, 1849, she powerfully presented the other side. Always a poised and eloquent speaker, Lucretia was at her best on that day. She held nothing back as she drew on her personal experience and her wide-ranging knowledge to speak passionately on women's position in society:

> There is nothing of greater importance to the well-being of society at large — of man as well as woman — than the true and proper position of woman. . . . This subject has claimed my earnest interest for many years. I have long wished to see woman occupying a more elevated position than that which custom for ages has allotted to her. . . . In the beginning, man and woman were created equal. "Male and female created he them, and blessed them, and called their name Adam." He gave dominion to both over the animals, but not to one over the other. . . . The laws given on Mt. Sinai for the government of man and woman were equal, [and] the precepts of Jesus make no distinction.

With these words, Lucretia laid to rest the accusations of her ecclesiastical contemporaries. She went on to name women throughout history who had excelled, despite prejudice and criticism, in the fields of education, science, social service, and the arts. Her own cousin from Nantucket, Maria Mitchell, was one of them. At a time when women were thought to be incapable of understanding scientific or mathematical theories, Mitchell had chosen to study astronomy. She had recently discovered a new comet, Lucretia announced proudly, and had become widely respected in her field.

Addressing the subject of marriage, Lucretia called for a union in which "the independence of the husband and wife will be equal, their dependence mutual, and their obligations reciprocal." She concluded by encouraging women to raise their expectations for success and to become more independent: "Credit not the old-fashioned absurdity, that women's is a secondary lot, ministering to the desires of her lord and master! It is a higher destiny I would award you."

"Discourse" was yet another milestone on the long and difficult road of social reform. It was perhaps the first time Lucretia had articulated, in a "carefully reasoned" but characteristically impromptu speech, all of her arguments in support of women's rights. A local reporter recorded the entire address, which was later printed as a pamphlet. Twenty years later, the pamphlet was still circulating, a reminder to women in both the United States and Great Britain that true equality was not a privilege but their "sacred right."

CHAPTER 10

Defending Females and Fugitives

On January 3, 1850, Lucretia Mott was fifty-seven years old. She had been a driving force in the anti-slavery movement for more than twenty years and a well-known Quaker minister for nearly thirty. She had fought many battles on behalf of those who occupied the lower rungs of society: women, slaves, and the poor. She had won most of these battles, and she expected to fight a few more — but less often. "The prospect of rest, even though not on laurels, is delightful," she told a friend. "It [is] . . . time for me to give place to the younger. Now that so many able women are in the [reforming] field, the 'gift' may be yielded to them without regret."

It would be more than a decade, however, before Lucretia could pare down her responsibilities and ease into semi-retirement. At this very volatile time in U.S. history, as women pushed forward in their struggle for equality and the argument over slavery reached its climax, her leadership and experience were needed more than ever. After her appearance at the Rochester convention and her highly successful "Discourse on Woman," she was regarded as the "guiding spirit" of the women's rights movement as well as the "elder stateswoman" of the anti-slavery cause. "Narrowness of purpose was impossible [for her]," writes biographer Margaret Hope Bacon. "She believed [that] if one were truly open to the leading of the Light, [then] all human rights were bound up in one by the indwelling Spirit."

The first National Woman's Rights Convention was held in Worcester, Massachusetts, in the fall of 1850. It was here that Lucretia met Lucy Stone, a young schoolteacher who was active in the anti-slavery movement. Like Lucretia, Lucy was quickly swept up in the fight for gender equality. The two became close friends, corresponding frequently throughout the next decade. Unlike Lucretia, however, Lucy chose not to divide her energies between causes. By the end of 1851, she had decided to "[devote] herself entirely to the woman's cause."

Meanwhile, Elizabeth Cady Stanton's influence in the movement was also increasing. Even while tending to her growing family in New York, she found time to promote women's rights through writings and speeches. Stanton maintained "a lively correspondence" with Lucretia, who was "the first woman she had known . . . who had sufficient confidence in herself to frame and hold an opinion in the face of opposition."

135

Although Lucretia was deeply devoted to her young friends and encouraged their ideas, she remained a somewhat reluctant leader of the women's movement. She was increasingly anxious to shed some of the overwhelming pressures and responsibilities associated with leadership in social reform. "As to 'taking a long breath,' it is what I have not done since the Convention of 1833 — rather since the separation in 1827 — indeed to speak the truth, since I was born," she confided to an acquaintance during this period.

In the thirteen years between the Seneca Falls Convention and the outbreak of the American Civil War, Lucretia would try many times to hand the reins of the women's movement to other younger women. Reformers such as Angelina Grimké, Lucy Stone, Abby Kelley Foster, and Susan B. Anthony had all become actively involved in the fight for equality during this time. But for all their intelligence and enthusiasm, it was Lucretia's presence, leadership, and continuing endorsement that gave this growing movement the respectability it needed to withstand the constant onslaught of ridicule and backlash.

Despite her "vehement objection," she was chosen to preside over the national women's rights conventions of 1852 and 1853. The former, held in Syracuse, New York, proved to be "a stormy and taxing" event. The sessions were attended by "several outspoken critics" who launched repeated verbal attacks on Lucretia and the other speakers. These men claimed that the women were "unfit for the roles they were assuming" and labeled them "immodest" attention-grabbers.

Lucretia and her colleagues did their best to ignore them. But when the men used passages of Scripture to bolster their arguments, Lucretia could no longer turn the other cheek. "The Bible has been ill-used!" she exclaimed. Her objection was supported by another reformer, Antoinette Brown, an ordained minister whose biblical knowledge matched Lucretia's own: Brown "introduced a resolution on the biblical justification" for women's rights. Lucretia, although she understood the heart behind the proposal, opposed it. Margaret Hope Bacon explains Lucretia's reasoning: "In the anti-slavery movement much time had been wasted by both sides claiming the Bible backed their position. It was better to let self-evident truth win its own arguments."

One gentleman in particular, the Reverend Junius Hatch, kept attacking the participants' "immodesty." Lucretia reproved him, but when he continued his comments despite her rebuke, "she called him to order sharply and told him to terminate his remarks."

After the convention, one Pennsylvania newspaper applauded the women's "firm and efficient control" of the meetings. But other newspapers were not as generous. "At Syracuse," wrote one New York reporter, " . . . the authority of the Bible as a perfect rule of faith . . . was voted down." Others referred to the convention attendants as "unsexed," "infidels," "offensive," and "militant."

The convention of 1853 was similarly volatile. It was held in early September in New York City, at Broadway Tabernacle near Worth Street. On the night of September 6, a mob broke up the convention, but the women remained composed. When Lucretia took the podium the following morning, she congratulated the women on their composure, their "self-reliance." And she herself was a shining example of such composure. In fact, as Margaret Hope Bacon points out, "No one else had the poise and authority to keep order nor the leadership to carry the frightened women through such ordeals." There was calm when Lucretia introduced the speakers, but as the day wore on, more and more "rowdies" came into the hall and interrupted the proceedings. By the time Sojourner Truth spoke that evening (she knew Lucretia well, having stayed with the Motts that spring), the hall was packed, and the troublemakers in the crowd were more unruly — so unruly that when the meeting was adjourned, "the hall exploded in confusion." When Lucretia noticed that some of the women were afraid to leave, she asked her own escort to take them out. When her escort asked her how she would make her way out of the building, she boldly took the arm of the troublemaker nearest her and said, "This man will see me through." And, remarkably, he did. It was no wonder that the women's movement looked to Lucretia for guidance and calm during these turbulent days.

Yet, in spite of constant ridicule and unending social

backlash, the early feminists continued to widen their sphere of influence. In addition to the annual conventions that were held, local women's rights groups gathered for regional meetings where they discussed issues and decided on possible courses of action. This grassroots activism attracted thousands of women nationwide who believed that "the proper sphere for all human beings is the largest and highest to which they are able to attain." They were convinced that no one segment of society had the right to decide for another segment "what is and what is not their proper sphere."

Gradually, women began to make strides both politically and professionally. New York was the first state to pass a law granting married women the right "to own and control property independent of their husbands . . . [the] right to wages earned by their labor [and] equal rights of guardianship over minor children." Women elsewhere lobbied heavily for the passage of similar laws in their own states. By the 1860s, many states had adopted this new legislation, which gave American women, for the first time, "some measure of control over their lives."

Through her letters and speeches, Lucretia encouraged younger women in their political activism. Yet she herself preferred to stay out of politics. Although she recognized that implementing women's newly won rights necessarily meant political involvement, she did not feel drawn into the arena of government. Instead, she devoted much of her energy to the improvement of opportunities for women in higher education and the professions.

In the "Discourse on Woman" speech she had delivered in 1849, Lucretia had stressed the importance of these opportunities: "Let woman then go on — not asking favors, but claiming as a right the removal of all hindrances to her elevation in the scale of being — let her receive encouragement for the proper cultivation of her powers, so that she may enter profitably into the active business of life." For Lucretia, this was not mere talk. She took her daughters to the first public health lectures given in Philadelphia. Only a few female medical students were present, but Lucretia was impressed by their knowledge, poise, and intellectual drive. Afterward, she enlisted the help of a Quaker businessman, William Mullen, and she and James helped Mullen and his wife (who was also interested in medicine) to raise money toward the establishment, in 1850, of the Female Medical College of Pennsylvania.

As the first institution of its kind in the country, it represented a giant step forward for women. Only a few decades earlier, women had been prohibited from studying or discussing human anatomy. "There was considerable question whether a modest girl could even study botany, learning about the male and female parts of the flower, without losing her delicacy," writes biographer Dorothy Sterling. Male medical students protested at the school's first commencement, "object[ing] passionately to the entry of females into the profession."

But intelligent, ambitious graduates like Dr. Ann Preston and Dr. Hannah Longshore were determined to pursue their careers despite the men's objections. The idea that female doctors were somehow less capable than their male counterparts persisted, however, and the women had difficulty attracting new patients. Brushing aside public criticism and superstition, Lucretia and other forward-thinking women placed themselves and their families in the women's care. Other families soon followed their example, and the women's practices grew steadily. Over the years, both Preston and Longshore earned reputations as skilled practitioners. In fact, "a few years later Ann Preston became the dean of the Female Medical College and the founder of Woman's Hospital in Philadelphia."

The Motts supported women entering other professions as well. They were among the primary fundraisers for the Philadelphia School of Design for Women (today known as the Moore College of Art), and they assisted the first female attorney in Pennsylvania in gaining admission to the required "bar" exams.

Inspired by female pioneers in science, medicine, and law, women all across America began to take their first tentative steps toward economic equality. "Women [had] found . . . a place in the working world and felt the intoxication of making a little money on their own," writes journalist Ishbel Ross. "[Finally], they had established a foothold, however precarious, in the great outside working world where men flourished."

Among these pioneers were Clara Barton, Dorothea Dix, and Graceanna Lewis. Barton, who later became famous as a Civil War nurse, founded the American Red Cross. Dix, who was superintendent of women nurses during the Civil War, became a widely recognized social worker who advocated prison reform and improved conditions for the mentally ill. Lewis began her professional life as a teacher, pursued scientific studies at Philadelphia's Academy of Natural Sciences, and later became "the country's foremost woman naturalist."

Throughout the second half of the 1800s, these women and others like them were pioneers in formerly "all-male" professions, serving as role models for subsequent generations. Lucretia promoted their efforts wholeheartedly, declaring that women's abilities had been "held in check" and that "a new generation . . . [was] now upon the stage." In fact, Lucretia's support was of fundamental importance. As Margaret Hope Bacon points out, "There is no question that her role was crucial in the development of the movement, not only for the obvious leadership she gave but for the nurturing care — the encouragement, the advice, the criticism — she provided to Elizabeth Cady Stanton, Susan B. Anthony, Lucy Stone, and a host of others whose names are now part of American history."

Although her involvement in women's rights took much time and energy, Lucretia continued to be the emotional cornerstone of her large, extended family. Several of James and Lucretia's children chose to raise their own families under their parents' roof, a fact that influenced the Motts' decision to move, in 1851, to a larger home on Arch Street. The running of such a large and lively household meant that Lucretia's flexibility, thrift, and organizational skills were in constant demand. In addition, her many domestic duties required a fair amount of physical work. But, as usual, Lucretia seemed to relish her homemaking tasks and her frequent stints as hostess. And she was now better equipped than ever to entertain. In her description of the new house, Margaret Hope Bacon notes that "here Lucretia had a thirty-foot-long dining room table for her immense dinner parties."

The move came shortly after James retired from the wool business. Although he was sixty-two and Lucretia was just a few years younger, they did not retire from their abolitionist activities, but remained devoted to the anti-slavery struggle. They welcomed visiting abolitionists into their home and frequently held anti-slavery meetings in their front parlor. Increasingly, these meetings focused on the consequences of the Fugitive Slave Act, whose passage in 1850 had alarmed many abolitionists. This act gave southern slave-owners the right to recapture blacks who had fled to the North and return them (often after severe physical punishment) to bondage. In addition, anyone who helped a slave to escape would be fined up to one thousand dollars and could serve between three and nine months in prison.

This new legislation was a giant step backward in

social reform and infuriated those who opposed slavery. Many who had ascribed to the "nonresistance" philosophy (made popular by abolitionist William Lloyd Garrison) were now forced to consider more active means of protest. These anti-slavery supporters, many of them Quakers, organized a secret system known as the Underground Railroad, which was designed to help fugitive slaves gain their freedom.

Traveling primarily at night, slaves journeyed to the North on foot or stowed away on hay wagons, stages, and trains. Under the guidance of abolitionists and other sympathetic citizens, they were shuttled to "stops" along several predetermined routes, and provided with food, shelter, and warm clothing. They remained hidden in barns, taverns, or private homes during the day, until darkness made it safe for them to continue their journey.

The Motts' home on Arch Street was one of the stops on the Underground Railroad. In addition to providing the fugitives with a temporary hiding place, warm meals, and clean clothing, the Motts were prepared to risk physical harm in order to defend the fugitives. On one occasion, a slave who had been flushed from his hiding place by his angry master dashed into the front door of the Motts' home, ran through the parlor, and hid in the back of the house. Witnesses say that James Mott "calmly stood at the door with a lighted lamp barring the [way]. He barely escaped death when [the angry master threw] a stone . . . past his head and [it] crashed into the side of the door."

In another episode, a former slave named Daniel Dangerfield was claimed by a Maryland plantation owner. Dangerfield, who had been free for several years and was employed near Philadelphia, was subsequently brought to trial as a fugitive.

Lucretia heard about the case and rallied support for Dangerfield. She marched into the courtroom with several of her friends and sat directly behind the defendant. The defendant's attorney, Edward Hopper, who was Lucretia's own son-in-law, called up "witness after witness to testify to Dangerfield's long residence in Pennsylvania."

All through the afternoon and into the evening, Lucretia and her friends sat patiently, focusing their full attention on the proceedings. Aware that the presiding judge was a devout Quaker, Lucretia spoke with him during the court's recess. "I earnestly hope that thy conscience will not allow thee to send this poor man into [bondage]," she said.

The judge, whose political supporters included pro-slavery advocates, appeared "more and more anxious" as the trial continued. Finally, one piece of evidence was introduced that allowed him to clear his conscience without ruffling too many feathers. Attorney Hopper read to the court a written description of Dangerfield provided by the plantation owner, stating that he was "five feet, nine inches tall." The official court measurement, however, found the defendant to be "five feet, ten inches tall in his boots and five feet, eight inches tall without them." With a sigh of relief, the judge declared Dangerfield a free man.

After the trial had concluded, witnesses crowded around Hopper and Dangerfield, expressing their congratulations. Many, however, credited Lucretia Mott's influence as the deciding factor in the verdict. "She was like an angel of light," said one man. "As I looked at her, I felt that Christ was there."

CHAPTER 11

So Many Lost

In 1856, just five years after their move to 338 Arch Street, the Motts decided once again to relocate. They bought a farm eight miles outside the city, directly across from property owned jointly by Thomas Mott and his brother-in-law, Edward Davis. "Roadside," as the main farmhouse was called, had been built in colonial times and needed repair. James did some of the work himself, then contracted stone masons, carpenters, and painters to finish the rest.

Throughout the winter of 1856 and into the spring of 1857, workers labored on the old farmhouse, adding "two roomy wings . . . a furnace in the cellar and a shower bath." (The Motts considered the latter a real luxury.) During this time, Lucretia made frequent trips to Roadside to inspect the workers' progress. With each visit, she became more attached to the property and gradually softened to the concept of country living. (Unlike James, who had often dreamed of being a farmer, Lucretia had initially opposed the move. But her children, who witnessed daily the demands put on their mother by needy individuals and various reform organizations, convinced her that it was a wise decision.)

In the early spring of 1857, James made "daily trips to the country with wagonloads of furniture," while Lucretia tacked down the new carpets and "haunted second-hand shops to find sofas and corner cupboards." In March, the workers left the farm. The last piece of furniture was removed from Arch Street and driven out to the country — the move was complete. To commemorate the occasion, Lucretia's children and grandchildren wrote a poem eulogizing their former home:

> Weep for the glory of 338!
> Weep for the family, once so elate!
> Weep for the friends who their sorrows will date
> From the day of the closing of 338!

But the farmhouse had much in common with the city home as far as family was concerned: the Motts' suburban household included various children, grandchildren, and an occasional niece or nephew, who lived with them for months or even years at a time. With daughter Maria across the road at Oak Farm and daughter Elizabeth and her husband Thomas Cavender occupying a summer house nearby, the family remained closely knit, and they supported one another through good times and bad.

The suburban experience was a new one for Lucretia; with the exception of her years at Nine Partners School, she had always lived in or near the center of town. Even in the fairly isolated community of Nantucket, she had lived within walking distance of her every need. Yet the countryside offered more privacy and the promise of days lived at a slower pace than was possible in Philadelphia. Far from city noises and the constant demands of visitors, neighbors, parishioners, and beggars, Lucretia gradually relaxed. Although she had never been particularly fond of landscapes or natural scenery (the beauty of the English countryside went unmentioned in her diary during her visit in 1840 to Great Britain), she was struck by the splendor and freshness of the surrounding fields, woods, and meadows. She took long walks around the farm and down Old York Road, noticing, perhaps for the first time, "the smell of the damp earth and the sparkle of dew on the grass." With James, she planted a vegetable garden and carefully pruned the overgrown orchard. When the fruit ripened, she left the choicest pieces on the wall beside the road so that passing children could enjoy them.

However, Lucretia made it clear from the beginning that, for her, the relocation should not be confused with retirement. She had no intention of severing ties with the various reform organizations to which she belonged, nor did she desire to become less active in local social groups. She corresponded frequently with colleagues in the anti-slavery and women's rights movements, and she continued to entertain reformers, writers, and lecturers involved in both. In addition, she remained an active and influential minister in the Society of Friends. "Despite Roadside's new satisfactions, Lucretia was in no danger of becoming countrified," writes biographer Dorothy Sterling. "On First Days the Motts drove to Meeting at Germantown. On Sixth Day evenings they walked 2 miles to Shoemakertown, where a group of local people had organized a debating society."

In addition to her new suburban activities, there were also "many errands to run in the city, Quaker Meetings and anti-slavery meetings to attend, shopping to do." Lucretia took advantage of the nearby Pennsylvania Railroad station, located just two miles down the road. Every few days, James or Thomas would drive her there in the horse-drawn cart and see her safely off. After the short ride to Philadelphia, Lucretia would spend the day running errands, visiting friends, and attending meetings.

She would return home in the late afternoon or early evening, laden with packages, groceries, and gifts for the grandchildren. Once, upon finding no one at the station to meet her, she carried the wooden high chair she had bought for her granddaughter all the way home. When Elizabeth spied Lucretia picking her way down the rutted country road, the chair balanced carefully on her head, she rushed out to help. Taking the chair, she admonished her mother for risking serious injury. "Heavens!" replied Lucretia with a wave of her hand. "It's not [at all] heavy!"

Besides maintaining many local involvements, Lucretia still traveled, sometimes to visit friends and relatives, sometimes to perform "public functions." In the fall of 1858 she went to visit cousins in Baltimore, preaching to a large group of blacks while she was there; when she returned to Roadside, Elizabeth Cady Stanton paid her a visit. In May of 1859, she presided over the Ninth National Woman's Rights Convention in New York (but not without protesting the appointment, as she had before). In November of 1860, after she and James "made their usual trip to Baltimore for the Yearly Meeting," they stayed on for a conference that focused on establishing a boarding school so that Hicksite boys wouldn't have to continue attending Haverford College, which was Orthodox. According to biographer Margaret Hope Bacon, "Lucretia and James were among those who insisted that the new institution, Swarthmore College, be coeducational."

The fall of 1860 brought the kind of pain and loss that Lucretia found so hard to bear: one of her grandchildren died of a gastro-intestinal disorder. It was the little girl of Lucretia's youngest child, Pattie; Lucretia did her best to comfort her.

In January of 1861, Lucretia celebrated her sixty-eighth birthday; shortly thereafter she was off to visit Lydia Mott, a cousin, who had invited her to a women's rights meeting being held in Albany. While in Albany, Lucretia, along with Elizabeth Cady Stanton and Ernestine Rose, went to speak to the New York legislature on the topic of divorce. Lucretia "made an impassioned speech," comments Margaret Hope Bacon, "saying that marriage was a sacred union between two people and the law had nothing to do with it at all. Let all the laws governing both marriages and divorce be swept away!"

This may have been a "radical" pronouncement, but Lucretia clearly knew what it took to sustain a marriage. In April of 1861, the Motts celebrated their fiftieth wedding anniversary. According to one relative's account, "several hundred friends gathered together at Roadside for the joyful occasion." The entire extended family, which now included a great-grandchild, was present for the reading of the original marriage certificate. When the document was presented during an informal ceremony, the guests speculated about the reason for its tattered appearance. Lucretia then explained, somewhat sheepishly, that she had used one of the corners to repair the children's badminton game some forty years ago. To further celebrate the milestone they had reached, James and Lucretia took a trip to Nantucket and visited her relatives there.

But the warm feelings that flowed from these celebrations were overshadowed by the beginning of the Civil War. Six southern states had seceded, electing Jefferson Davis as their "provisional" president. In the months that followed, five more states would join them, forming their own confederacy and pitting "brother against brother" in the bloodiest battle the nation had ever known.

Lucretia's reaction to the conflict was predictable. The war, she believed, was "the natural result of our wrong doings and our atrocious cruelties." Although she abhorred violence, she knew that the "deep-rooted tension" between the North and the South, particularly on the issue of slavery, must somehow be resolved. "Let us hope it will not be stayed by any compromise which shall continue the unequal, cruel war on the rights and liberties of millions of our unoffending fellow beings," she said.

It didn't take long for the realities of war to touch the family. Several of the younger Mott men enlisted, and many of the sons, brothers, and nephews of Lucretia's closest friends were commissioned into service. The threat of these potential losses was heightened by an actual loss at Roadside: Lucretia's granddaughter Anna died of tuberculosis at the end of 1861. Lucretia dealt with her grief in a tried-and-true way: she immersed herself in a new task. Margaret Hope Bacon recounts that "Lucretia began a project that she was to continue throughout the war: gathering clothes and raising money for the freedmen. At first she did this on her own. Later she helped to organize a Women's Association for the Aid of the Freedmen at Race Street Meeting."

Abraham Lincoln's Emancipation Proclamation of January 1, 1863, freed the slaves in "rebel areas" but "specifically exempted all areas under federal military occupation and did nothing to disturb slavery in the loyal border states." Lucretia considered the proclamation a step in the right direction, but she was disappointed in the president's reluctance to grant immediate and total abolition. She referred to Lincoln as "a miserable compromiser" and reminded her anti-slavery colleagues that their struggle was not over.

That same month, the northern (Union) Army set up a training camp for black soldiers in the fields adjacent to Roadside, calling it "Camp William Penn." From her parlor window, Lucretia watched the soldiers drill, lamenting the fact that "so many young and strong" would be sacrificed to peace. In the ensuing months, she visited the camp frequently, bringing homemade pies and gingerbread to the enlisted men and supplying the camp's cook with fresh produce from Roadside's garden and orchards.

The Mott family was not untouched by the war. A young Coffin cousin was killed, and another wounded; and in early summer, Willie Wright, one of Lucretia's nephews, was badly hurt. When he was well enough to be moved, he was sent to Roadside to recover.

On July 12, 1863, Lucretia accepted an invitation to speak by the commanding officer of Camp William Penn. Standing "on a drum so she could be seen by the six hundred soldiers," she addressed the entire camp: "The time will come when war [will] be no more," she assured them. Her optimism helped to keep the soldiers' spirits high despite grim accounts of bloody battles waged in Virginia, Maryland, and central Pennsylvania.

Throughout all this, Lucretia remained a steadfast pacifist. Later that year, when she spoke to the Philadelphia Female Anti-Slavery Society, she supported "the loftier position of those who fought only with the spiritual weapons and endured without inflicting injury."

The war dragged on for more than a year. On April 9, 1865, Confederate General Robert E. Lee surrendered to the Union Army at Appomattox, Virginia. On May 26, the last Confederate regiment surrendered in Shreveport, Louisiana — the Civil War was over. Like most American families, the Motts celebrated the return of peace. But with 600,000 dead and thousands of once able-bodied men crippled for life, Lucretia remained unconvinced "that there was any such thing as a just war." Lincoln's assassination on April 14, which troubled her deeply, reinforced her belief that violence in any form was evil and that humankind must rely increasingly on "moral weapons" to resolve differences.

The war was over, but Lucretia's daughter Elizabeth was losing her battle with cancer. She had begun to go into a decline in 1863, when her fourteen-year-old son died. Lucretia nursed her at Roadside until her death on September 4, 1865. Again, Lucretia's grief was deep: "A lovely link in our circle was removed from us by death," she wrote to a friend.

But the year 1865 also held other victories besides the war's end. The Thirteenth Amendment to the Constitution abolished slavery nationwide. Abolitionists rejoiced, but some remained skeptical that blacks, though free, would truly enjoy equal rights in a racially mixed society. Lucretia was one of those who claimed that "the mere abolition of slavery . . . did not mean that the Negro would automatically obtain the full rights of citizenship." She supported the continuation of the American Anti-Slavery Society, which she believed should function as a watchdog agency for the enforcement of the rights of blacks.

When the majority of members voted to disband, however, the Motts joined the newly formed Association for the Aid and Elevation of the Freedmen. This organization, sponsored by the Society of Friends, was established to "[help] the American Negro obtain the education required by free citizens of a democratic republic, and to lobby for congressional enactment of civil rights legislation on [their] behalf."

In keeping with their commitment to nonviolence and the fostering of good relationships among all people, the Motts helped to establish the Pennsylvania Peace Society early in 1866. A "predominantly Quaker society," it was "dedicated to the outlawing of war as an instrument of national policy." Its members believed that education was the key to the peaceful resolution of conflicts, and that acquiring nonviolent habits began in the home. Consequently, "they were opposed [to] using tax monies for the military, training young men to be soldiers, and glorifying war. . . . [They] denounced physical punishment, military drilling and warlike toys."

Meanwhile, Lucretia continued to fight an individual

battle against discrimination. She regularly relinquished her comfortable seat inside horse-drawn cars and stood outside on the platform designated for blacks. When the property adjacent to Roadside (fomerly Camp William Penn) was sold for development, she insisted that the new neighborhood be racially integrated. The result was one of the first mixed-race communities, named "La Mott" in Lucretia's honor.

Increasingly, Lucretia's reform efforts centered on the well-being of free blacks. In place of the annual antislavery fair, Lucretia and her daughters organized fundraisers for black orphanages and schools for the children of the freedmen. They collected clothing for displaced families and helped them to secure adequate housing and meaningful employment. They paid monthly visits to the Stephen Smith Memorial Nursing Home, a retirement facility for blacks (which Lucretia had helped found), bringing the residents "scrapple and [home-]baked pies."

Throughout the 1860s, equal rights for both women and minorities continued to be a pressing national issue. In May of 1866, "a group met in New York to form the American Equal Rights Association." The goal of the organization was to lobby for the rights of all citizens, regardless of class, race, age, or gender. At the request of Elizabeth Cady Stanton, Lucretia agreed to act as president, saying that she "would be happy to give her name and influence if she could encourage the young and strong to carry on the good work."

At seventy-three, Lucretia remained both intellectually and socially active, serving as a mentor for the next generation of social reformers. In the writings and speeches of Susan B. Anthony, Lucy Stone, and Stanton, she was still referred to as "saint," "angel," and "lioness." Lucretia responded to these compliments with characteristic humility: "I am a much overrated woman," she confided to her family. "It is humiliating!"

The equal rights movement grew in influence, so Lucretia was perplexed by the blatant gender discrimination in the proposed Fourteenth Amendment. The new legislation extended voting rights to all *male* citizens, causing many feminists to become "thoroughly alarmed." Not all women's rights advocates were in favor of demanding suffrage, however. Several conservative members of the women's movement, including Lucy Stone and Abby Kelley Foster, preferred to avoid the suffrage issue in favor of education and employment reforms.

Eventually, disagreement over the right to vote caused a split in the women's movement. Lucretia was exasperated: "I weary of [their] everlasting complaints," she wrote to her sister Martha. As in the past, she played "the thankless role of peacemaker," attempting to appease those on both sides of the argument. Despite her best efforts, however, the women remained polarized.

The constant infighting took its toll on Lucretia's physical health; she looked tired and began rapidly losing weight. And the death of her daughter still weighed heavily on her heart. Her family became concerned and decided that a brief vacation might prove "restorative."

Thus, in August of 1866, Lucretia traveled to Nantucket, accompanied by her daughters Anna and Maria. Her spirits rose almost immediately. She visited old friends and enjoyed meals at the homes of distant relatives, rekindling fond memories of her childhood, her parents, and the peaceful Quaker community where she had spent her formative years. Despite recurring bouts of nausea (her digestive troubles increased as she aged), she relished samples of the island's specialties: clams, oysters, blackberry pie, and corn pudding. She enjoyed long, solitary walks on the beach and stood for hours watching "the heavy surf on the south shore."

She returned to Philadelphia, having gained a few pounds and feeling more rested than she had in months. But this physical improvement didn't last long: Lucretia felt ill much of that fall and winter. She remained fairly active, but sometimes just felt too poorly to participate in the meetings others pleaded with her to attend.

By the spring of 1867, however, Lucretia's health was improving. In May of that year she went to the second annual meeting of the American Equal Rights Association, "where she presided again as president." Factions in the group were still fighting about the Fourteenth Amendment, but Lucretia was equal to the challenge. Just a few weeks later, she attended the founding convention of the Free Religious Association. It was composed of men and women of various denominations who were "dedicated to the promotion of brotherhood among America's numerous religious groups and to a general uplifting of the moral tone of society." Although Lucretia didn't actually join the organization for several years ("she objected to a phrase in the society's constitution"), she was "thoroughly in sympathy" with it. And, unlike other larger organizations to which Lucretia belonged, this smaller society remained free of disruptive arguments that might have otherwise weakened it.

Lucretia and James spent the summer of 1867 at Roadside — the last summer they would spend together. In January of 1868, James caught a cold that developed into pneumonia. Lucretia and her children did what they could to help him, but within a week it was clear that James would not recover.

Early on the morning of January 26, 1868, James Mott breathed his last. For Lucretia, his wife of fifty-six years, life would never be the same again.

CHAPTER 12

Fading Light

After James's death, Roadside was inundated with letters from Lucretia's friends and colleagues all over the United States and Great Britain. Even those who opposed her ideas — including some well-known conservative clergymen, politicians, and writers — put aside philosophical differences to express their heartfelt sympathy.

Lucretia was "numbed" by her husband's passing. She "wandered disconsolately from room to room," trying to comprehend the reality of his absence. James had been her friend, lover, and personal adviser for nearly six decades; like the victim of a sudden amputation, she would sometimes act as if he were still there: "Scarcely a day passes that I do not think, of course for the instant only, that I will consult him about this or that," she told a close friend.

And yet, unlike the deaths of her infant son Tommy and her grown daughter Elizabeth, James's passing at the age of eighty seemed somehow more natural, more in tune with the cycle of human life. In her letters dating from that period, Lucretia refers to "James's long life with me" and calls him "the [old] glory of Roadside."

Her children and grandchildren rallied to support Lucretia as she grieved. Respecting her more frequent need for solitude, they took care of the house and grounds and sat with her while she read by the fire on cold February evenings. Granddaughter Fanny Cavender stayed at Roadside, keeping out-of-town family members apprised of Lucretia's health and helping to answer the mountains of sympathy letters that were still pouring in.

Before James's death, Fanny had planned to marry Tom Parrish on the Motts' wedding anniversary. Out of respect for her grandfather's passing, however, she thought it best to postpone the ceremony. But when Lucretia learned of this, she became indignant: "Thou will do no such thing!" she told Fanny. "'Twill give me joy to share my happy day with you!" The wedding took place as planned on April 10, 1868, at Roadside. The ceremony proved cathartic for Lucretia, who "wept unashamedly . . . with tears of tenderness."

In the weeks that followed, Lucretia seemed restored to her usual cheerfulness. She began appearing in public more frequently, taking trips to the city, and speaking out at the local Friends Meeting. At home, she continued her lifelong habit of reading and began making new "scrap" carpets for her grandchildren. In several of these, she sewed pieces of brightly colored material that Elizabeth Stanton had sent her, along with a poem:

Lucretia Mott, my dearest friend
This day to you a box I send
Containing gifts so bright and rare
I warn you to unpack with care. . . .

Ofttimes I have wished myself
Some horrid man, a bird or elf,
But now I'd be a scarlet rag
To live forever in thy carpet bag.

Stanton also kept her friend informed of the progress being made in the women's movement. But Lucretia remained befuddled and disappointed over the continuing disagreements within the group itself. As a result, she focused increasingly on the more general cause of peace.

Following the example of Quaker Alfred Love, who had formed the Universal Peace Union in 1866, Lucretia made the cause of peace her "most consuming interest." (Besides serving as vice president of the union, Lucretia also — according to Love's diaries — publicly addressed the subject of peace no less than forty times in the last decade of her life.) In 1869, she spoke at the Unitarian Church in Washington, D.C. Standing before "a crowd of elegantly dressed women, dignified senators and representatives [who] stood side by side with plainly clad working men and women," she made her case for nonviolence. Despite the horrors of the recent Civil War, Lucretia exhorted her listeners to "take a cheerful view of the past . . . [and] be hopeful for the future," using only "moral weapons" to settle conflicts. A reporter from the *Lewiston Journal* (Maine) wrote, "So inspired by love of humanity was all she said, that each one present felt his heart throb and glow with nobler thoughts, higher inspirations and deeper love to his fellow men."

Many of Lucretia's sermons during this time contained a message urging "work and an active religion." Rhetoric had its place, she said, but people needed to commit themselves to a life filled with works inspired by faith. Only then, she believed, would they truly follow in the footsteps of Jesus Christ: "This formal waiting upon the Lord . . . sitting still may be abused. . . . Active labor is better, for that IS waiting upon the Lord," she told the Washington gathering.

In the fall, Lucretia helped prepare for the opening of nearby Swarthmore College (named after the residence of George Fox, founder of the Quaker religion). James Mott had served on the original board of managers that had established the school by written charter in 1864. Unwilling to delegate this "piece of unfinished business" to someone outside the family, Lucretia took his place, serving as an adviser to the board. Upon learning that her daughter Anna Hopper had been appointed to the new board and that several of the Mott grandchildren were "considering enrolling as students," Lucretia rejoiced. Education had been one of James's foremost preoccupations in his later years; Lucretia felt sure that he would be proud to have left such a legacy.

Opening ceremonies took place in October. As a memorial to her late husband, Lucretia brought two young oak trees that James had "started from acorns" at Roadside. Several hundred people gathered at the tree-planting ceremony, which was "accompanied by speeches and photographs." Lucretia obliged willingly when asked to say a few words. After expressing her high hopes for students enrolled at the new co-educational school, she urged them not to forsake their spirituality. According to biographer Margaret Hope Bacon, she warned them of the "skepticism that sometimes grows out of the study of science when unaccompanied by religious faith."

In February of 1870, Lucretia lost her sister Eliza to pneumonia. She dealt with her grief as she usually did: by immersing herself in causes. The very next month she gave the farewell speech to the Philadelphia Female Anti-Slavery Society, which was disbanding. In April, although she was tired of the infighting in the women's rights movement, she was drawn into the role of peacemaker for a meeting intended to reconcile the two conflicting groups. (The meeting was unsuccessful, though Lucretia did her best.)

That year also saw Lucretia elected president of the

Pennsylvania Peace Society. She would hold this post for the next ten years, waging a personal campaign against violence in all of its forms. She made her most dramatic plea in 1873, after several Modoc Indians who "had been resisting forced settlement in California" were captured and sentenced to death. When she learned that President Grant was visiting a wealthy financier who lived near Roadside, she decided to make a personal call on the president to intercede on the Indians' behalf. President Grant actually received Lucretia, and he "listened thoughtfully to her earnest pleas."

Lucretia turned eighty-one in 1874, a year that brought a dark crop of deaths in her circle of friends and family. A few years earlier, Marianne, her sister Martha's daughter, had died; so had a great-grandson. But 1874 brought even more losses. Her longtime friend Miller McKim fell ill in March and died in June. That spring, Lucretia's daughter Anna learned she had a tumor in her throat; she died in August. The very next month, Anna's son Isaac died. The crowning blow came when Lucretia's sister Martha died of pneumonia just a short time later.

For a while after that, Lucretia thought she herself might die. But once again she managed to weather these shocks by turning to family, friends, and causes.

On April 14, 1875, Lucretia was an honored guest at the centennial celebration held by the Pennsylvania Abolition Society (the all-male organization that James had previously served as president). Henry Wilson, vice president of the United States, gave her a glowing in-

troduction: "I . . . present to you one of the most vener-
able and noble of American women, whose voice for
forty years has been heard and tenderly touched many
noble hearts. Age has dimmed her eye and weakened
her voice, but her heart, like the heart of a wise man
and wise woman, is yet young."

Although Lucretia remained intellectually sound, her
physical health declined with age. She lost weight, and
she continued to have difficulty with her digestion. She
accepted this affliction rather stoically, however, and
simplified her daily diet to include coffee, bread, pudding, and peas. She still rose early in the morning and
could often be found in the garden with "a floppy
sunbonnet on her head and a basket over her arm . . .
pick[ing] peas . . . or raspberries for her family to enjoy
at breakfast."

In the summer of 1876, Lucretia made a final journey to her birthplace on Nantucket. At age eighty-three,
she was one of her generation's oldest survivors, a fact
that did not disturb her in the least. When a relative
pointed out that she had exceeded her expected life-
span, Lucretia quipped, "It's better not to be in a hurry
with obituaries." Still stubbornly independent, she even
refused to be escorted across the uneven cobblestone
streets. "I learned long ago to lean on myself," she told
a young man who had offered assistance.

The vacation was a time of healing for Lucretia. The
restful days spent on Nantucket allowed her to remember the loved ones she had recently lost and to let go

of the pain she had carried with her from their untimely deaths.

In 1878, when she was eighty-five, Lucretia traveled to Seneca Falls to attend the thirtieth anniversary of the first Woman's Rights Convention. Family members worried that the meetings would prove too strenuous for her, but Lucretia wrote to them saying that she felt "rejuvenated." At the convention, she spoke "at length," saying, "Give woman the privilege of cooperating in making the laws, and there will be harmony without severity, justice without oppression." Veteran abolitionist Frederick Douglass and feminist Belva Lockwood (the first woman to practice law before the Supreme Court) also spoke in favor of women's suffrage, equal pay for equal work, and improved educational opportunities.

At the end of the two-day session, Lucretia stepped off the platform to a standing ovation. Her back was bent with age, and wisps of white hair stuck out around the sides of her bonnet. As she walked slowly toward the exit, many in the audience wept, feeling sure that this would be her last public appearance.

During the last two years of her life, Lucretia did remain closer to home. Still surrounded by family members, she found contentment in simple daily pleasures such as gardening, sewing, reading, and conversing with friends. On her eighty-sixth birthday, she received a letter from the managers and employees of the Pennsylvania Railroad, who expressed their gratitude for her many years of patronage. "A happy continuance and peaceful ending of [your] long and useful life," they wrote affectionately.

Despite frequent ill health, Lucretia continued to take the train into town to attend meetings of the Philadelphia Peace Society. According to one member's account, she "often spent the entire day [in the meeting room], eating soda crackers and resting between sessions."

The 1880 meeting of the Peace Society's Executive Committee was her last. Now a frail eighty-seven years old, Lucretia remained confined to Roadside. By autumn, she spent most of her waking hours in her room, where she was visited frequently by her remaining children, grandchildren, great-grandchildren, nieces, nephews, and a few close friends. Sensing that the end was near, she requested that her funeral service be a simple one. "Mine has been a simple life," she reminded her family. "Let simplicity mark the last done for me."

On November 11, 1880, Lucretia Coffin Mott died peacefully in her sleep. A small memorial service was held at Roadside, but several thousand mourners gathered for her burial at Fair Hill cemetery, overlooking the city of Philadelphia. After a few words from a member of the Peace Society, an intense silence fell over the crowd. Finally, one man whispered, "Will no one speak?" Another replied, "Who can speak? The preacher is dead!"

❂   ❂   ❂

Today, Lucretia Mott's portrait (painted by Joseph Kyle in 1841) hangs in the National Gallery in Washington, D.C., among those of the most influential men and women in our country's history. Her likeness is etched in stone, alongside that of Susan B. Anthony and Elizabeth Cady Stanton, in a statue (sculpted by Adelaide Johnson in 1921) that stands in the crypt of the U.S. Capitol. Her letters, her diary, and the transcripts of her speeches are housed in several of our most prestigious libraries and universities.

But much more important than these tangible legacies is the current manifestation of Mott's lifelong work in social reform. Although there is still plenty to be done, much of the progress that has been made on the issues of women's rights, racial tolerance, and world peace has its roots in the nineteenth-century movements in which Lucretia played a pivotal role.

For Lucretia Mott, the development of a decent society was a creative act — always in progress, ever flexible, subject to changes in human needs and perspectives. Today, her struggle continues, for there are some who claim that the life patterns of human beings are fixed and thereby justify a rigid social hierarchy based on race, religion, and gender. If she were alive today, Lucretia would surely tell them, "Thou had better think again!"

My Sources for This Book

Among the several dozen sources that I consulted in researching and writing this book, a few were particularly helpful. *James and Lucretia Mott's Life and Letters,* edited by Mott's granddaughter Anna Davis Hallowell (Houghton, Mifflin, 1884), provided many of the direct quotations that appear throughout the text. Otelia Cromwell's *Lucretia Mott* (Harvard University Press, 1958), Dana Greene's *Lucretia Mott: Her Complete Speeches and Sermons* (Edwin Mellen Press, 1980), and Dorothy Sterling's *Lucretia Mott: Gentle Warrior* (Doubleday, 1964) were also very useful. Margaret Hope Bacon's lively and thorough book *Valiant Friend: The Life of Lucretia Mott* (New York: Walker & Co., 1980) provided me with the most current information on Mott's life. Excerpts from *Valiant Friend* are found frequently here, and I gratefully acknowledge Bacon's permission to use this material.

I would also like to thank Betsy Brown, librarian at

Haverford College in Haverford, Pennsylvania, for her assistance in locating and using critical documents from the Quaker Collection. These included first-edition copies of Hallowell's *Life and Letters* and *Slavery and the Woman Question: Lucretia Mott's Diary of Her Visit to Great Britain,* edited by Frederick Tolles (Friends' Historical Society of Haverford, Pennsylvania, 1952).

Suggestions for Further Reading

Archer, Jules. *Breaking Barriers: The Feminist Movement from Susan B. Anthony to Margaret Sanger to Betty Friedan.* New York: Viking Press, 1991.

This is a well-written, thoroughly researched book that traces the history of feminism from its beginnings to the 1980s. The book contains a wealth of interesting information that Archer presents in an easy-to-read style.

Bacon, Margaret Hope. *Quiet Rebels: The Story of the Quakers in America.* Philadelphia: New Society Publishers, 1985.

Written by one of the nation's leading Quaker scholars, this book gives an excellent overview of Quaker history. Bacon provides a thorough chronicle of the evolution of the Society of Friends, from its early British roots to its present philosophy and commitment to social activism.

Bacon, Margaret Hope. *The Story of Quaker Women in America*. San Francisco: Harper & Row, 1986.

This is an excellent account of how Quaker women have influenced such issues as civil rights, gender equality, and nonviolence. It contains biographical profiles of many prominent women who were pioneers in social activism during the colonial and Civil War periods. The book is written for adults, but it is accessible enough for most teenage readers.

Clarke, Mary Stetson. *Bloomers and Ballots: Elizabeth Cady Stanton and Women's Rights*. New York: Viking Press, 1972.

Details of the first Women's Rights Convention as well as portraits of several early feminists are found in this fine volume, written for young adults.

Harper's Ferry Historical Association. *Frederick Douglass: An American Life* (video). West Virginia: H.F.H.A., 1984.

This film biography gives an accurate portrait of the fugitive slave who later became a famous public speaker, writer, and civil rights advocate. It includes re-enactments of his encounters with William Lloyd Garrison, Harriet Tubman, and John Brown.

Lerner, Gerda, ed. *The Female Experience: An American Documentary.* New York: Oxford University Press, 1977.

This collection of original documents and letters is arranged according to women's natural life cycle, from birth to old age. Each section is preceded by an essay that focuses on the particular life stage being featured, with Lerner's analysis of how each has evolved through the past few centuries. This book is appropriate for both teenage and adult readers.

Sawyer, Kem Kapp. *Lucretia Mott: Friend of Justice.* Massachusetts: Discovery Enterprises, Ltd., 1991.

This lively picturebook for younger readers, which contains charming illustrations, highlights the main events in Mott's public and private life. Former First Lady Rosalynn Carter provides an introduction.

Index